AF451199

ClarityPeak
Publishing

Published by ClarityPeak Publishing, Düpheid 61, Hamburg, Germany

Printed by various print service providers worldwide.

ISBN:
978-3-911416-00-9 Paperback
978-3-911416-01-6 Hardcover
978-3-911416-02-3 eBook

Book Cover Design: Katarina Naskovski

First Edition: June 2024

BEYOND OVERWHELMED

10 STEPS TO A PURPOSEFUL AND EMPOWERED LIFE

DAVID CHRISTIANSEN

For everyone on a journey to find their best self.
May you find the strength and inspiration you need.

**You can't stop the waves,
but you can learn to surf.**

– Jon Kabat-Zinn

CONTENTS

INTRODUCTION

NAVIGATING THE STORM: UNDERSTANDING STRESS IN THE MODERN WORLD

Before the sun even peeks over the horizon, you are already thinking about the long list of things you need to do. From the moment you wake up, it's a rush—checking messages, preparing breakfast, and gearing up for a busy day. Stress sneaks into your life like an uninvited guest. It affects everyone. Even though it's a shared experience, it's often lonely. It makes you feel as though you're battling it alone.

THE WEIGHT OF THE WORLD: RECOGNIZING OUR SHARED STRUGGLE

Imagine being stuck in traffic. You watch the minutes tick away as you're trying to get to an important meeting. Your heart pounds, your hands grip the steering wheel tighter, and a flood of worries fills your mind. You might think this story is personal. But it's a daily reality for millions. Recently, global anxiety and depression have spiked, revealing stress as a common health issue. Recognizing this is the first step towards changing how we deal with these pressures.

In my travels, including a year spent living on another continent, and conversations with people from diverse cultures around the world—such as a profound exchange with an Aboriginal elder in Australia—I've navigated the vast landscapes of human experience. Hello, I'm David Christiansen. As a father of three and a professional tasked with orchestrating complex projects under pressure, I've learned to master the delicate balance between high-stress professional environments and the demands of home life.

This journey has been fueled by listening to people, meditation and a relentless pursuit of knowledge on how to live more meaningfully. I've encountered intense periods of overwhelm—from managing critical moments that required precise coordination to handling the simple yet profound anxieties of daily life. These experiences have not only shaped my understanding but have also ignited my passion to assist others. This book emerges from my desire to share the insights I've garnered, offering strategies to manage stress and transform challenges into opportunities for growth and happiness.

"Beyond Overwhelmed" is your compass in the chaos of everyday life. This book is designed to provide you with practical steps and transformative knowledge for profound personal change. Whether you're tackling daily stress, seeking deeper connections, or aiming to redefine your life's path, the journey begins here.

CHAPTER ONE

UNDERSTANDING STRESS AND ITS IMPACT

There I was, hands gripping the steering wheel with such intensity that my knuckles turned white. My heart pounded as if trying to escape my chest. I was crossing a bridge—a mere structure of steel and concrete, yet in those moments, it felt like a passage through my deepest fears. Each time, the experience was the same: a visceral fear of the depths below, a terror of the endless fall that never came. This fear extended beyond heights, reflecting the deep sense of vulnerability I experienced following a significant loss in my life. It manifested most acutely as I drove over bridges, transforming these crossings into trials by panic.

As my family sat in the car, oblivious and chatting merrily, I wrestled silently with my racing thoughts, the pressure building relentlessly. Each time I made it across, I felt a quick moment of happiness, but then another bridge would appear, and the fear came back. From now on planning routes became a tactical challenge to avoid any bridge, and if unavoidable, I'd reluctantly pass the wheel to my wife. Her presence, her hand on mine, was my anchor, a calming force that gently pulled me back from the edge of panic.

This episode was a profound revelation about the pervasive power of stress and anxiety. It underscored the necessity of recognizing these invasive moments, confronting them head-on, and mastering them to reclaim tranquility and command over my life. Each bridge I crossed became a personal milestone, a testament to overcoming the immediate pressures that once seemed insurmountable.

Stress, that sneaky guest in our busy lives, doesn't wait for an invitation to show up. It jumps on us when we least expect it, often at times when we're simply trying to meet the next personal goal or navigate the day's challenges. It's something we all face, but it hits everyone differently. Think about it: a ticking clock as a deadline approaches, a disagreement that heats the air, or the daily rush to work can easily send us into a state of panic. Noticing these moments is key to taking back control and finding our calm again.

But figuring out what exactly makes us stressed isn't easy. Stress weaves its way through our day-to-day life so sneakily that identifying its root cause feels like trying to solve a complex puzzle. This hidden struggle impacts us both mentally and physically, leading to nights where sleep just won't come, muscles that won't relax, or a fuse that's a bit too short. What makes tackling stress even tougher is that it doesn't look the same for everyone, making the search for a universal cure pretty much impossible. So, understanding stress is not just about knowing it's there but really getting how it affects us in deep and diverse ways.

UNVEILING PERSONAL STRESS TRIGGERS

Stress is like a shadow that constantly follows us around in our busy lives. It's important for us to pay attention and deal with it. Sometimes, we're so caught up in life that we don't even notice what's really bothering us. The first step to getting out of this cycle is to figure out what exactly makes us feel so restless. What stresses us out can be different for everyone, from tight deadlines at work to unexpected changes at home. Knowing what these stress triggers are not only gives us power but also gets us ready to face stress when it comes.

Imagine being able to predict a storm coming; if you know it's on the way, you can find shelter before it hits. But finding out what makes us stressed isn't always easy. A lot of times, these triggers hide in our everyday routines and are hard to spot. This is where writing down what stresses us out can really help. Keeping a record helps us see patterns or themes in what gets to us. If you're thinking about starting such a journal, here's what you can do:

- Write down any time you feel upset or anxious, even if it seems small.

- Record how you react physically, emotionally, and what you do in response.

- Look back at what you've written every so often to spot any patterns or common triggers.

This straightforward method shines a light on the stressors we often miss and helps us tackle them more effectively (Sparks, 2019).

It's also key to understand how we each react to stress since everyone handles it differently. Some people might get headaches or feel tired, while others might become irritable or pull away from people. Getting to know how we respond to stress is crucial for coming up with ways to cope that work for us personally. This awareness acts like a guide, showing us healthier ways to handle stress.

Not all stressors are created equal. Some things we can control and others, we just can't. Knowing which is which is really important. It allows us to focus our energy where it can actually make a difference. For example, we might not be able to fix a bad economy, but we can control how we react to it and take steps to look after our finances. Here's how we can practically apply this knowledge:

- For things you can change, come up with steps to deal with them head-on.

- For things outside your control, work on being more resilient and managing your stress response instead of trying to change the unchangeable.

Taking this balanced approach to managing stress not only improves our current situation but also prepares us for future challenges.

Understanding and managing stress is a very personal journey that takes time and commitment. Learning that not all stress can be gotten rid of — but can be managed — is freeing. It encourages us to be proactive with stress, seeing it not as a huge barrier but as something we can navigate through as part of our life.

At the heart of becoming strong against stress is knowing ourselves better. By identifying what stresses us and how we react, we can start making positive changes. Using coping strategies that fit our own needs can change how we live day to day, moving from constantly fighting against stress to living in balance with it.

Mastering stress isn't about getting rid of it entirely; it's about learning to live with it in a way that it doesn't control us. Changing how we view stress doesn't happen overnight. It's a slow process that happens as we get better at noticing how we react to stress and using coping methods that really work.

Embarking on this journey requires bravery, dedication, and a curiosity about our inner worlds. Imagine navigating a winding road—there are ups and downs, unexpected turns, but each step forward is a step toward liberation from unmanaged stress, leading us toward a richer, calmer existence. Picture yourself learning to dance with the challenges: sometimes stepping forward, sometimes back, but always moving with grace and resilience. Our happiness and health depend significantly on how flexibly and understandingly we navigate life's stressful moments. By honing these skills, we not only uplift our own lives but also radiate positivity to those around us.

Practical Exercise: Stress Trigger Journal

- For one week, write down situations that cause you stress, noting your thoughts, feelings, and reactions.

- At the end of the week, review your entries and look for patterns or common themes in your stress triggers.

- Reflect on how you can apply the stress management strategies discussed in this chapter to better handle these triggers in the future.

THE BODY UNDER SIEGE: CHRONIC STRESS EFFECTS

Chronic stress sneaks up on us, quietly weaving its way into our lives, and it's often too late when we notice how much it's affecting our physical health. Our bodies react to stress in ways that can lead to some serious health troubles like heart issues, weakened defenses against germs, and stomach problems. It goes beyond just feeling "stressed out." We're talking about the real deal here – how stress not only messes with our minds but also harms our bodies. Think about it: when stress sticks around for too long, it puts our systems into overdrive, messing up pretty much everything from our hearts to our hormones. This constant state of alert can increase our chances of facing things like heart attacks, high blood pressure, and strokes ("How stress affects your health, n.d.").

It doesn't stop there. Chronic stress can mess up our sleep, change our weight, and even make it harder to think clearly. Our bodies, trying to handle stress, shoot up levels of cortisol and adrenaline. These are the "get ready to run or fight" hormones that are super useful if there's an actual physical danger. But when what's stressing us out is all in our heads, these hormone changes can mess with our sleep, make us put on weight, and make it hard to remember stuff. These issues aren't small potatoes; they can really drag down how well we live our day-to-day lives and get things done.

Then there are the signs stress is getting to be too much, like headaches, muscle knots, and just feeling wiped out. These symptoms are not just bothersome. They're like flashing lights warning us that stress is doing a number on our health. They push us to remember how important it is to keep our minds and bodies in harmony.

Knowing all this, it becomes crucial that we start taking steps to reduce stress's impact on us. This can be as simple as learning to relax more or as involved as seeking therapy. Here are a few pointers to help ease the tension:

- Make exercise a regular part of your routine to help lower stress.

- Get into a good sleep groove by going to bed at the same time each night.

- Find peace with mindfulness or meditation practices.

- Hanging out with friends or joining a group can make you feel less alone.

- And if stress gets too heavy, talking to a professional can offer you strategies tailored to your needs.

Tackling chronic stress involves more than just addressing the symptoms; it requires considering the whole picture, both mind and body. The connection between mental and physical health is tight. Problems in one area can lead to trouble in another, showing why it's so important to deal with stress comprehensively.

A big step in handling stress better is simply admitting it's there and understanding how it can mess with our health. Too often, we brush off stress as just a part of life. However, considering the damage it can do, it's time we take it more seriously. It's vital for everyone – from bosses to doctors to each of us – to work towards spotting stress early and making managing it easier.

Just because life moves fast doesn't mean we're doomed to be stressed out. Knowing how stress affects us physically gives us the power to choose healthier ways to cope. We owe it to ourselves to put our health first, to build up the strength to meet life's ups and downs without letting stress wear us down.

So, what's next? We've got to face stress head-on, push for mental health to be taken seriously, and back up research into beating stress. By doing this, we're not just making our own lives better; we're helping to create a society that's happier and more productive.

Personal Example: Jake's Battle with Chronic Stress

Jake, a 45-year-old project manager, found himself constantly under the gun. With deadlines looming and client demands skyrocketing, his days were a blur of back-to-back meetings and late-night emails. At first, he brushed off the persistent headaches and the mounting pressure in his chest as mere nuisances, assuming they were just part of getting older.

But then, one morning, Jake woke up with a start. His heart was pounding furiously, and he felt an overwhelming sense of dread. At work, while preparing for a major presentation, his vision blurred and his thoughts scrambled. This wasn't just another busy day; it was a full-blown panic attack. Rushed to the hospital, Jake was stunned when the doctor linked his symptoms not just to an isolated incident but to a pattern of chronic stress that had been taking a toll on his body for years.

Forced to take a medical leave, Jake reflected on the signs he had ignored—constant fatigue, irritability, insomnia, and now, a scare that shook his very foundations. Determined to regain his health, he began a comprehensive stress management program. He prioritized regular exercise, adopted a meditation routine, and made significant changes to his diet. Most importantly, he learned to delegate tasks at work and set firm boundaries to ensure he had time to unwind.

Months later, Jake's health had improved dramatically. His experience was a wake-up call to his colleagues and family, highlighting the severe consequences of unchecked stress. It made everyone more aware of the need to take proactive steps to manage their stress effectively.

COPING MECHANISMS FOR IMMEDIATE RELIEF

Jake's story highlights the profound impact chronic stress can have on both mind and body. His journey from relentless pressure at work to a complete breakdown illustrates how untreated stress can escalate into severe health issues. But his recovery journey also shows the power of holistic approaches to managing stress, integrating both mental and physical health strategies.

Just like Jake, many people face chronic stress daily. Understanding that tackling stress involves more than just addressing its symptoms is crucial. It requires a comprehensive approach that considers the entire picture – both mind and body. In this chapter let's explore effective strategies to manage chronic stress, drawing from both personal experiences and scientific insights.

In our bustling world today, it's pretty common to bump into things that stress us out, affecting our peace of mind. Luckily, we've got some techniques and tools ready to help us deal with these moments more smoothly. Practices like deep breathing exercises, easing our muscles through progressive relaxation, and staying mindful are right at our fingertips to help keep our stress levels in check. These methods bring us back to the now, making the stress seem less overwhelming. Here's a simple guide on how you can make use of these tools:

Deep Breathing

Deep breathing is a basic yet powerful technique for stress relief. It may sound simple, and indeed it is, but it's always beneficial to be reminded of the basics. Deep breathing helps calm your nervous system, reduces stress hormones, and brings you back to the present moment. Here's how you can practice deep breathing:

1. **Find a Comfortable Position**: Sit or lie down in a comfortable position with your back straight.

2. **Inhale Slowly**: Breathe in deeply through your nose, allowing your abdomen to expand fully.

3. **Hold Your Breath**: Pause for a moment to hold the breath.

4. **Exhale Slowly**: Breathe out slowly through your mouth, letting go of any tension.

5. **Repeat**: Continue this process for a few minutes, focusing on your breath and the sensations in your body.

It's good practice to repeat this exercise regularly, especially during stressful times. Consider setting aside a few minutes each day or using it as a quick stress reliever whenever you feel overwhelmed.

Progressive Muscle Relaxation

Building on deep breathing, progressive muscle relaxation is an excellent way to release physical tension and calm your mind. This technique involves tightening and then relaxing various muscle groups throughout your body. Here's how to practice it in more detail:

1. **Start with Deep Breathing**: Begin by practicing a few minutes of deep breathing to center yourself.

2. **Feet and Toes**: Focus on your feet and toes. Tighten the muscles by curling your toes downward and hold the tension for about 5 seconds. Then, slowly release the tension while breathing out, noticing the sensation of relaxation.

3. **Calves**: Move up to your calves. Tighten the muscles by pointing your toes upward, hold for 5 seconds, then release while exhaling.

4. **Thighs**: Tighten the muscles in your thighs by squeezing them together. Hold for 5 seconds, then release and relax.

5. **Abdomen**: Contract your abdominal muscles, hold for 5 seconds, then slowly release.

6. **Hands**: Clench your fists tightly, hold for 5 seconds, then release.

7. **Arms**: Tighten your biceps by drawing your hands towards your shoulders, hold for 5 seconds, then release.

8. **Shoulders**: Shrug your shoulders up towards your ears, hold for 5 seconds, then let them drop and relax.

9. **Face**: Scrunch up the muscles in your face by squeezing your eyes shut and tightening your mouth. Hold for 5 seconds, then release.

As you go through each muscle group, remember to breathe deeply and focus on the feeling of relaxation that follows the release of tension. This practice not only reduces physical tension but also brings a sense of calm and peace to your mind. Some people find that meditative music enhances their relaxation, while others achieve deeper focus with minimal distractions.

Mindfulness

With a foundation of deep breathing and progressive muscle relaxation, mindfulness can further enhance your ability to manage stress. Mindfulness involves paying attention to the present moment without judgment. It's about observing your thoughts and feelings from a distance, without getting caught up in them.

This practice can significantly reduce stress and improve overall well-being.

Whether you choose to meditate or simply focus more on the experience of everyday activities like eating or walking, mindfulness paves the way to peace and clarity. In the following sections, we will delve deeper into mindfulness and other effective techniques to manage stress, providing you with a comprehensive toolkit to navigate the challenges of daily life.

Easily Accessible Stress Reduction Techniques

Other helpful methods to reduce stress include getting active, spending quality time outdoors, or letting calming music wash over you. These options are simple and easily accessible. Engaging in physical activity releases endorphins, natural mood enhancers that can brighten your day. Spending time outdoors lowers stress hormones, boosts your mood, and sharpens your mental clarity. Walking barefoot on grass or soil for a few minutes each day can effectively change your stress levels. As well Music has a remarkable ability to soothe the soul, providing immediate relief from stress. Its gentle power can transform our mood, offering a peaceful escape from daily pressures.

Reaching out to friends for support plays a crucial role as well. Sharing your burdens with someone you trust can offer not just comfort, but a fresh outlook—something we all need when times get tough. It means having a space where you're free to be open about your worries, assured that you'll find understanding and warmth.

Building a personal set of strategies for dealing with stress is incredibly empowering (Can et al., 2020). It means picking and mixing different tactics to discover what's most effective for you.

Whether it's exercising, writing down your thoughts, enjoying hobbies, or practicing relaxation techniques, the goal is to build a dependable toolkit for yourself. This prepares you to effectively manage stress whenever it arises.

Having a variety of ways to handle stress not only improves our immediate responses but also strengthens our resilience over the long haul. It acknowledges that while stress is part of life, we're not powerless against it. Adopting this outlook can significantly enhance our mental and emotional health, fundamentally changing how we view and interact with stress. No longer is it something to dodge at all costs, but rather a chance to grow and learn.

STRATEGIES FOR LONG-TERM STRESS MANAGEMENT

Stress, that annoying tag-along in our speedy lives, does more than make us frown. It can really mess with our health, both in body and mind, showing us how important it is to find ways to keep it under check. Let's walk through some effective, long-lasting methods to lessen stress, aiming for a life filled with more smiles and less worry.

Having a strong daily routine plays a big part in fighting off stress. This means making time for exercise, eating well, and getting plenty of sleep. These simple steps are key to managing stress daily. Exercise does more than benefit your body—it acts as a natural mood enhancer by boosting feel-good chemicals, improving your mood, and helping you relax for a better night's sleep. Similarly, eating right is essential; nutritious foods provide the strength your body needs to tackle stress effectively. And on the subject of sleep, sticking to a regular bedtime is crucial. A set sleep schedule keeps your internal clock in check, leading to less stress all around.

Here's how to weave these basics into your lifestyle:

- Make moving your body a must-do, whether it's a quick jog, calming yoga, easy exercises like push-ups, abdominal workouts, or even fitness sessions with a VR headset. While 150 minutes a week might sound like a lot, it breaks down to just about 20 minutes a day.

- Choose fresh, whole foods over the processed stuff, ensuring a diet that backs up your stress-fighting powers.

- Get into a solid sleep rhythm by hitting the hay for 7-9 hours each night and establish a pre-sleep ritual to tell your body it's time to slow down.

Diving into activities like meditation, yoga, or tai chi can also make a huge difference in handling stress. These practices bring us back to emotional center, cutting down anxiety and boosting our sense of well-being by keeping us focused on the here and now. This ability to stay present helps us take a step back from stress, giving us a moment to choose our reactions wisely and lowering our stress levels (Staff, 2021).

Getting started with relaxation techniques can be easy:

- Set aside a little time each day for meditation or yoga—even ten minutes can do wonders.

- Try out different relaxation methods to discover what fits you best; maybe it's guided imagery, progressive muscle relaxation, or deep breathing.

- Look into apps or online videos that offer a guiding hand through meditation (for example *Headspace*) or yoga (for example *Yoga For Beginners*).

Adding to our stress-busting tools, setting doable goals, getting savvy with how we use our time, and not being shy to ask for expert advice when necessary are also key. These strategies help tackle not just the symptoms of stress but its root causes, letting us manage our time and tasks without feeling swamped.

To streamline your time and dial down stress:

- Chunk up tasks into smaller bites and sort them by urgency and importance.

- Craft SMART (Specific, Measurable, Achievable, Relevant, Time-bound) goals for clear guidance and focus (Mayo Clinic, 2022).

- Recognize when it's time to reach out for help, tapping into community resources or counseling for support and new ways to cope.

The cherry on top of our stress management plan involves fostering a sunny outlook, indulging in hobbies or activities that light us up, and nurturing our social ties. When we dive into things we love, from painting to reading or hanging out with dear ones, we shift gears away from stress towards something positive. Just as importantly, keeping up with friends and family provides emotional backing that's priceless when times get tough.

To cultivate a life filled with joy:

- Carve out time for fun and games, making sure they're a fixed part of your week.

- Embrace gratitude by taking a moment to appreciate the good in your life, changing how you see daily stresses.

- Grow your circle by staying in touch with friends and family and welcoming new people into your life.

KEY STRATEGIES FOR NAVIGATING
THE STRESS LANDSCAPE

Through our journey exploring stress, its origins, and how it infiltrates our wellbeing, we've come to a powerful realization: tackling stress is not only essential, it's entirely achievable. Remember our initial comparison of stress to an unwanted visitor. It's time we stood up for ourselves, learning to coexist with it without allowing it to dominate our lives.

We've looked closely at what personally triggers our stress, the heavy burden prolonged stress places on us physically, and the refuge offered through immediate and long-term methods for managing stress. We find ourselves at a pivotal moment. Moving forward isn't about trying to completely get rid of stress—that would be an endless struggle. Instead, it's about feeling empowered and resilient. This understanding prepares us not only to face today's stress but also to tackle whatever challenges might come our way tomorrow.

It's vital to see that our individual battles with stress have a wider impact, touching the lives of those in our communities and places of work deeply. By each of us taking steps to handle our stress better, we start a chain reaction, creating spaces where openness, support, and overall health are cherished and promoted.

SUMMARY

- **Identifying Stress:** Learn how stress enters our lives unexpectedly, affecting everyone differently, from students to working professionals.

- **Recognizing Symptoms:** Explore how everyday situations like traffic jams, work deadlines, or technological overload contribute to our stress levels.

- **Personal Experiences:** Gain insights from my (the author's) own struggles with stress, including anxiety on bridges and the challenges of daily responsibilities.

- **Importance of Awareness:** Understand the significance of acknowledging your stress triggers as the first step towards effective management.

- **Practical Strategies:** Begin to explore strategies such as deep breathing, progressive muscle relaxation, mindfulness, simplifying your routine, and setting realistic expectations to help reduce stress.

- **Encouragement for Action:** Motivate yourself to take the first steps toward reclaiming your calm by recognizing and addressing the stressors in your life.

CHAPTER TWO

THE POWER OF MINDFULNESS IN DAILY LIFE

Life moves at an incredibly fast pace these days. It's as if we're on a non-stop treadmill, where days meld into each other and precious moments just slip through our fingers like sand. Ever felt that? Just going through the motions without really absorbing the wonderment around you? Imagine then, being able to hit 'pause' on this fast-forward life. Imagine taking a moment to truly soak in the now, cherishing every little miracle that comes your way. This is what mindfulness brings to the table—a serene island in our otherwise storm-tossed lives. It invites us to not just exist, but to live fully and embrace each moment with all our being.

However, welcoming mindfulness into our lives isn't a walk in the park. In a world that puts a trophy on doing ten things at once, and where our senses are relentlessly flooded with data, breaking news and new developments, carving out a quiet corner for ourselves seems almost unthinkable. The effort to mute the endless chatter in our heads and the constant hum of the world around can leave us feeling more alienated than ever. This sense of disconnection pulls us into a whirlpool of stress, worry, and the overwhelming feeling that everything is just too much. And thus, we find ourselves trapped in a vicious cycle that feels impossible to snap out of.

This section of our journey together is about softly steering you towards a state of harmony and awareness. By embracing the art of mindfulness, you'll discover how to achieve emotional balance and harness the strength that comes from living in the present. By simply paying attention to your breath, listening to what your body is telling you, and watching your thoughts as they come and go without passing judgment, you will learn to tread life's roller-coaster with a newfound grace. Within these pages lies a treasure trove of wisdom and actionable steps to weave mindfulness seamlessly into your daily life. Picture transforming mundane tasks into chances for personal growth and deeper connection. Gradually, you'll uncover the joy of a life lived with intention, centeredness, and genuine happiness.

HARNESSING MINDFULNESS FOR EMOTIONAL EQUILIBRIUM

Stepping into the world of mindfulness might feel like a big jump at first, especially when life seems to rush by, pulling our thoughts from past regrets to future worries. However, there's a wealth of scientific proof out there showing that mindfulness is a powerful tool. It's not simply a brief break from the chaos; it's actually a key to improving our overall quality of life.

Mindfulness has an incredible power to anchor us in the here and now. It goes beyond enjoying the present moment by also reducing stress and clearing the fog in our minds. This, in turn, sharpens our thinking. In today's world, where doing ten things at once is often applauded, our ability to concentrate gets chipped away, leaving us feeling scattered and drained. Mindfulness brings us back to the now—whether through focusing on our breathing, noticing how our body feels, or observing our thoughts without passing judgment—helping us build a defense against the urge to overthink or worry.

It also plays a huge role in helping us manage our emotions better. By becoming more aware of ourselves, we not only spot what sets off our emotions but also become less likely to snap under pressure. Instead of being tossed around by life's ups and downs, mindfulness gives us a moment to breathe and choose how we want to react. It reminds me of a wise saying: "Between stimulus and response there is a space. In that space is our power to choose our response. In our response lies our growth and our freedom." Mindfulness broadens that crucial space, offering us the freedom to choose and the strength to weather emotional storms with grace.

The peace and quiet mindfulness brings into our lives goes a long way in boosting our well-being. It's like the calm after a storm, where stillness brings insight and renewal. This sense of peace is not just about relaxing but about setting a new baseline of calm from which we can approach the world more effectively. It dials down the constant buzz of stress, helping us see what's truly important in our lives with greater clarity.

Let's not overlook the positive impact mindfulness has on our relationships. It teaches us to listen carefully and to speak with kindness and understanding. By doing so, it deepens our connections with others and enhances mutual respect and empathy. Just imagine how this could transform a whole community, creating an atmosphere of support and shared understanding.

All these advantages add up to a more balanced and mindful way of living. And yes, studies back this up. Research cited by (What are the benefits of mindfulness?, n.d.) points out that mindfulness is linked to reduced overthinking and stress, as well as improvements in how flexible our thinking is, the quality of our relationships, and various health outcomes. This evidence highlights the broad and positive effect mindfulness can have on our minds, hearts, and even our social lives.

The beauty of mindfulness lies in its simplicity: just being fully in the moment and accepting it without judgment can work wonders. Despite its straightforward nature, the effects can be deeply transformative.

By embracing mindfulness, we're not just finding a way to calm our minds or ease our worries in solitude. We're opening doors to a fuller way of living, rich with engagement and awareness. It's about realizing the vast potential each moment holds for discovery, growth, and connection. And in a time when everything seems to move faster and faster, having a grounded sense of mindfulness is like having a personal refuge, a peaceful spot within that we can come back to anytime.

INFUSING EVERYDAY ROUTINES WITH MINDFULNESS

Starting your day with a bit of mindfulness meditation can really change the vibe of your whole day. It's not about just sitting quietly; it's about getting ready for what the day has in store. Giving yourself just a little time each morning to focus on your breathing and being in the moment not only offers you some peace but also gets your mind ready to handle whatever comes your way with better focus and patience. You can use the exercises from the previous chapter as a starting point. The same study I've mentioned before found additionally that people who practice mindfulness feel more mindful, dwell less on repeated thoughts, and generally feel more positive (What are the benefits of mindfulness?, n.d.). It's pretty amazing how something so simple can make such a big difference in our day-to-day life.

Life throws stress at us all the time but reacting to it with mindfulness can really change the game. Using deep breaths as a tool helps us stay anchored in the present, making it easier to deal with stressful times more gracefully.

Deep Breath Extended Technique

Let's go back to our Deep Breath exercise and extend it. Whenever you feel overwhelmed, simply stop for a moment. Remind yourself that you know this helpful technique and start.

Let me ask you one thing: When was the last time a situation or a person stressed you out and you didn't have the right reaction at hand? Sometimes, we just have to escape from the situation because we can't handle it. Feel free to stop reading for a moment, think back, and find a situation like this.

Now let me show you a technique that can help you calm down and step back for a moment.

1. **Inhale Slowly**: Breathe in deeply through your nose, allowing your abdomen to expand fully.

2. **Hold Your Breath**: Pause for a very short moment and hold the breath.

3. **Inhale Once More**: Fill your lungs to their maximal capacity.

4. **Hold Your Breath**: This time, hold it for a longer duration.

5. **Exhale Slowly**: Breathe out slowly through your mouth, letting go **of** your stressful situation.

Wait a moment before allowing your breath to naturally draw in again.

Repeat this a few times. This two-breath technique can provide an even deeper relaxation. Feel free to experiment with both methods (Deep Breath and Deep Breath Extended) to discover what works best for you in different situations.

Do you remember my bridge-crossing problem from the beginning of the book? This is an example of a situation where the Deep Breath Extended technique rescued me in the midst of traffic on a huge bridge, while I thought my life was collapsing. I could calm down a bit, gain some perspective, and continue driving with a clearer mind.

Additionally mindfulness doesn't have to be a solo act; you can set up little reminders around you to keep mindfulness at the top of your mind throughout the day. Something as easy as setting alarms with notes like "Take a mindful moment" or sticking notes around with reminders to breathe or observe carefully what's around you. These little hints encourage us to pause and bring ourselves back to the present, weaving mindfulness into our daily life bit by bit.

Bringing mindfulness into our everyday tasks introduces a level of awareness and serenity that benefits us and those around us. It changes normal moments into chances for being truly present, altering how we experience life one step at a time. Mindfulness's simplicity and its deep impact on how we feel emotionally and on our overall health are truly beautiful. So why not give it a shot? By integrating these practices, you are moving through your day with purpose and appreciation in each moment.

Mindfulness is all about taking small, intentional steps to stay present and engaged, no matter what we're doing, be it eating, walking, or just breathing. Every mindful moment counts, adding up to a clearer and calmer state of mind. This isn't just hopeful thinking—there's solid research showing the vast benefits of mindfulness, from reducing stress to bettering relationships and sharpening our mental functions (What are the benefits of mindfulness?, n.d.).

By adopting mindfulness, we improve our own lives and also play a part in creating a kinder, more attentive world. It's about taking charge of our emotional health and recognizing our ability to positively shape our experiences. As someone who values personal freedom and the well-being of society, I believe mindfulness is a powerful tool that can help improve the world—one thoughtful breath at a time.

Practical Exercise:
Mindful Morning Routine

- Set aside 10 minutes each morning for a mindfulness practice.

- Begin with a few minutes of deep breathing, focusing on the sensation of the breath moving in and out of your body.

- Engage in a mindful activity, such as sipping tea or stretching, paying close attention to the sensations and experiences of the present moment.

- Reflect on how starting your day with mindfulness affects your overall well-being and ability to handle stress throughout the day.

EATING MINDFULLY

Now, let's chat about eating mindfully. Mindful eating is about truly savoring every bite and being present during your meals. When we eat without distractions and pay attention to the flavors, textures, and how the food makes us feel, we digest our food better and enjoy our meals more.

The Benefits of Mindful Eating

Mindful eating helps us appreciate the nourishment our food provides and fosters a healthier relationship with what we consume. By focusing on each bite, we become more attuned to our body's signals of hunger and fullness, leading to better portion control and increased satisfaction from smaller amounts of food.

Steps to Eat Mindfully

1. **Eliminate Distractions**: Turn off the TV, put away your phone, and create a calm environment for your meal. This helps you focus solely on the eating experience.

2. **Appreciate Your Meal**: Before you start eating, take a moment to look at your meal. Appreciate the colors, textures, and effort that went into preparing it. This simple act can increase your gratitude and enjoyment.

3. **Take Small Bites**: Instead of rushing through your meal, take smaller bites. This allows you to fully experience the flavors and textures of the food.

4. **Chew Thoroughly**: Chewing well aids digestion and slows down your eating pace, giving your body time to signal when it's full.

5. **Engage All Your Senses**: Use all your senses to enjoy your food. Notice the aroma, the taste, the sound of the crunch, and the feel of the food in your mouth. This multisensory experience enhances the pleasure of eating.

Making Eating an Event

When you practice mindful eating, meals transform into enjoyable events that provide a moment of peace and connection with yourself. By fully engaging in the act of eating, you build a healthier, more appreciative relationship with your food, leading to better overall well-being.

Mindful Eating in Practice

Think of mindful eating as a practice that you can incorporate into your daily life. Start with one meal a day, dedicating time to fully engage with your food. Over time, this mindful approach becomes a natural and rewarding habit, fitting seamlessly into your lifestyle.

Why Mindful Eating Matters for Sarah and John

For Sarah, the Aspiring Marketing Manager, mindful eating can enhance her busy life. By taking time to savor her meals, she creates pockets of calm in her hectic schedule, helping her recharge and maintain balance between her professional ambitions and personal well-being.

For John, the Creative Freelancer, mindful eating offers a way to bring structure to his flexible yet chaotic routine. By making meals a focused, sensory experience, he establishes a rhythm that helps him separate work from personal time, fostering a healthier work-life balance.

ENHANCING RELATIONSHIPS THROUGH MINDFUL COMMUNICATION

Understanding how to communicate mindfully in our relationships can feel like solving a puzzle. At first glance, it looks complicated, but it really boils down to something simple yet incredibly impactful. Mindful communication extends beyond the words we exchange; it involves being fully present, showing kindness, and listening without judgment to each other's thoughts and feelings. In today's fast-paced world, where quick replies are often valued more than careful thought, this way of interacting isn't always our go-to. However, embracing this approach opens up a new depth of connection and understanding with the people in our lives.

The Foundation of Mindful Communication: Active Listening

The foundation of mindful communication is active listening. This means giving our full attention to the person speaking, making an effort to understand them, responding in a thoughtful way, and remembering what they've said. Sounds easy, right? But think about how many times we start thinking about our response while the other person is still talking.

Here are some tips for getting better at active listening:

- Pay complete attention to the speaker and try to put your own thoughts on pause.

- Use your body language and small verbal affirmations to show you're engaged.

- Summarize their points to make sure you've got it right.

- Hold off on judging so you can really grasp where they're coming from.

- Take your time to respond thoughtfully.

Personal Example: Lisa's Inclusive Leadership

Today Lisa, a manager, notices her team member, Eric, seems quieter than usual during meetings. Instead of assuming he's disinterested, she uses active listening during their one-on-one. She pays full attention, nods, and occasionally repeats back a summary of what Eric says. This approach helps her discover that Eric feels his ideas might be overshadowed by more vocal team members. Understanding his concern, Lisa acknowledges his feelings and discusses potential strategies to ensure everyone's voice is heard in meetings.

Growing Compassion in Communication

Being compassionate in how we respond is another key part of mindful communication. It's about seeing the emotions behind someone's words and answering with kindness and support. Even when we may not fully agree, dealing with the situation from a place of care strengthens our connections. To grow in compassion:

- Try to feel what the other person is experiencing and understand the feelings behind their words.

- Speak in a way that shows you get it and are there for them.

- If you can, offer help or solutions that come from a genuine desire to make things better for them.

Personal Example: Jenna and Rob's Wedding

Jenna and Rob are navigating the stresses of planning their wedding. When Rob expresses frustration about the growing costs, Jenna takes a moment to understand his concerns instead of dismissing them as overreaction. She responds with empathy, acknowledging that they both want a beautiful day but need to be mindful of their budget. Together, they review their plans, showing mutual support and understanding, which not only resolves the tension but also strengthens their bond.

Offering a Judgment-Free Space

Offering a judgment-free space where everyone feels safe to open up is vital. When we hold back our snap judgments, we show acceptance for the whole person, flaws and all. This kind of support makes both people feel valued and deepens their bond. Practicing this means:

- Noticing our immediate reactions and pausing to reflect before we speak.

- Recognizing our own biases and consciously putting them aside.

- Making it clear that it's okay to share, reinforcing that their thoughts and feelings are welcome.

Adopting mindful communication in our everyday interactions brings many rewards. It can make our relationships stronger, help us solve disagreements peacefully, and lay a foundation of trust (Forster, 2017). This approach leads to a cycle of positive exchanges, fostering deeper, more meaningful connections. Plus, it spreads kindness and empathy, affecting not just our personal relationships but also the larger community around us.

Forster (2017) highlights that mindfulness in how we talk to each other is especially beneficial in romantic partnerships. Being there, tuned into each interaction, recognizing our partner's needs without rushing to judge, and responding with warmth and comprehension all play a role in nurturing a happier, more satisfying relationship. This research emphasizes how important it is to incorporate mindfulness into our daily conversations, highlighting its power to improve both personal satisfaction and the strength of our relationships.

Choosing to communicate mindfully doesn't mean we'll never face conflicts or tough emotions again. Rather, it's about approaching these natural parts of life with calmness and care. It involves making an active choice each day to listen intently, speak gently, and keep our hearts open.

In an era where division feels rampant, mindful communication shines as a ray of hope. It reminds us that the essence of every interaction is the chance for connection and understanding. By dedicating ourselves to mindful communication, we enhance our own lives and make strides toward a kinder, more empathetic world.

MINDFULNESS TECHNIQUES
FOR STRESS MANAGEMENT

Starting a journey toward better emotional stability and being more present in the moment is like learning to sail on unpredictable waters. Imagine being a sailor who stays calm and focused despite the ever-changing ocean. Similarly, anyone dealing with life's ups and downs can find stable ground through mindfulness. It isn't about avoiding tough times but learning how to move through them with strength and elegance.

Mindful breathing is a simple yet powerful starting point – we have talked about it. In stress-filled situations your pulse quickens, and thoughts whirl around your head. This is where focusing on your breath comes into play - it's like an anchor you always carry with you. Taking slow, deep breaths tells your body to relax, balancing out the stress hormones flooding your system. This effectiveness in bringing peace to both mind and body is supported by research (Mindfulness meditation: A research-proven way to reduce stress, n.d.), proving its ability to create calm in the storm.

Adding to the peaceful effects of mindful breathing, the practice of a body scan helps too. It means gently going over each part of your body in your mind, from head to toe, paying attention to tension without trying to change it. It's similar to the Progressive Muscle Relaxation technique we already know, but a bit different, as you this time just notice your feelings of each part of your body and they might start to ease up. This method has helped many people relax in real, noticeable ways by encouraging them to look inward and let go of hidden stresses.

Moreover, becoming mindfully aware of our thoughts and feelings can change our reaction to life's roller coaster. This approach doesn't involve ignoring our discomfort but observing our inner experiences without rushing to judgment. By giving ourselves room to think before we act, our reactions can better reflect our true values, not just impulsive emotions. This practice deepens our self-understanding and encourages a kinder perspective towards our own experiences.

Grounding techniques are also essential, especially when feelings or situations feel too intense. Simple actions like focusing on the sensation of your feet on the ground or noticing the details around you can snap you back to the present moment. These strategies work as beacons of light, guiding you through the fog of overwhelming stress. Far from being just figurative speech, they are real, practical ways to stay centered amid life's commotion. For example, this can also help if you are afraid of flying and being in the air: Notice your feet on the ground of the airplane. This personally helped me many times when I had some medium anxiety about flying. This simple grounding technique can be very helpful. Just give them a try and feel free to combine them with the breathing techniques.

Each of these practices—mindful breathing, body scanning, observing thoughts and feelings, and grounding exercises—is a step toward handling stress more lightly and living more balanced. They're not arbitrary tips but are backed by solid research showing their success in supporting mental health (Maya et al., 2021). Mindfulness invites us into a new relationship with life, characterized by embracing the moment and accepting rather than dodging our experiences.

Learning these mindfulness techniques is similar to picking up any new skill. It might seem odd or hard at first, but with persistence, these methods become more familiar, changing not just how we cope with stress, but improving our overall quality of life. The goal isn't constant calm—that's not realistic—but to have the right tools ready for when life's rough waves hit.

Mindfulness isn't a cure-all solution, and it's important to keep expectations in check. Benefits develop over time and can vary by person. Yet, there's strong evidence that it helps build emotional strength and mental toughness. This book aims to provide you with practical and effective mindfulness techniques that you can start applying right away. By incorporating these methods into your daily routine, you'll find it easier to manage stress and enhance your overall well-being. While there are many additional resources available—through classes, online, or do-it-yourself guides—the strategies and practices outlined here are designed to give you a solid foundation to build upon.

The push for mindfulness goes beyond personal growth; it's about setting the stage for healthier communities and society. As more people learn to manage their emotions and stress, the impact can lead to more patience, empathy, and kindness all around. Therefore, the widespread adoption of mindfulness could change how we interact with one another, improving social bonds and community spirit.

EMPOWERING LIVES
THROUGH MINDFULNESS

Embarking on this mindfulness journey together has revealed a remarkable tool that helps us gracefully steer through life's ups and downs. Amid the hustle and bustle that fills our days, as well as those quiet instances filled with hidden messages, mindfulness stands as a beacon, helping us stay grounded. It's all about welcoming each moment with an open heart and a peaceful mind, no matter what it brings.

Do you recall our discussions about the breakneck speed of everyday life? That overwhelming sensation of being stuck on a cycle that never seems to end isn't a fixed state. By embracing mindfulness, we've learned to step out of that endless loop and engage with the world around us, keeping our balance and calm even in chaos.

This transformation may seem modest at first glance, yet its ripple effects are profound, touching not just our lives but also reaching the hearts and minds of those around us. By choosing mindfulness, we're not only altering our own existence; we're weaving a web of empathy, patience, and kindness within our communities.

SUMMARY

- **Benefits of Mindfulness:**

  - **Emotional Equilibrium**: Mindfulness helps manage emotions and stress, enhancing emotional balance and reducing the overwhelming feelings that arise from modern life pressures.

  - **Enhanced Concentration**: Practicing mindfulness counters the fragmentation of attention caused by multitasking, improving focus and mental clarity.

  - **Improved Relationships**: By fostering patience and empathy, mindfulness enhances interpersonal relationships and communication.

- **Practical Steps for Integration**:

  - **Mindful Breathing**: Simple exercise to focus on breathing to reduce stress and center oneself in the present.

  - **Mindful Eating**: Encourages eating without distractions, savoring food, which aids better digestion and satisfaction with meals.

  - **Daily Mindfulness**: Incorporating mindfulness into daily routines like morning or evening rituals to maintain a constant state of awareness and presence.

- **Impact on Well-being**:

  - **Personal Growth**: Regular mindfulness practice leads to personal development and a deeper connection with oneself.

  - **Community Impact**: Mindfulness can foster a more empathetic and understanding community, improving social bonds and interactions.

- **Mindful Communication**:

  - **Active Listening**: Emphasizes the importance of truly listening to others without judgment, enhancing understanding and connection.

  - **Compassionate Response**: Encourages responding to others with empathy and kindness, facilitating stronger and more positive relationships.

- **Mindfulness Techniques for Stress Management**:

  - **Stress Management Tools**: Use techniques like the body scan and grounding exercises to manage daily stress and maintain emotional stability.

- **Living a Mindful Life**:

  - **Continual Practice**: Mindfulness is not a one-time solution but a lifelong practice that enriches everyday experiences and enhances quality of life.

  - **Community and Personal Health**: Promote the adoption of mindfulness across communities to improve overall social and emotional health.

CHAPTER THREE

BALANCING WORK AND PERSONAL LIFE

I magine it's a typical Monday morning. Laura, a project manager, finds herself sipping coffee while responding to work emails on her phone, even before she gets out of bed. As she prepares her kids for school, her mind races through the day's meetings. Even during her commute, she's on calls, and at home, her laptop often competes with family dinner. This constant tug-of-war between her professional responsibilities and her personal life leaves her feeling like she's failing at both. Laura's experience is not unique; it echoes the struggles of many trying to find that elusive work-life balance in today's non-stop world.

Laura's story highlights a widespread dilemma: how to balance the increasing demands of our professional lives with our personal well-being and family responsibilities. This balancing act impacts our overall health, happiness, and productivity significantly. To manage this, it's crucial to establish boundaries that protect our personal time, allowing us to disconnect from work and truly engage with our lives outside the office.

Strategies for achieving a better work-life balance include setting specific work hours and adhering to them, even when working from home. It also involves being intentional about taking breaks and scheduling time for activities that rejuvenate us—be it exercise, hobbies, or spending time with loved ones. Furthermore, leveraging technology smartly—like turning off notifications outside of work hours—can help maintain these boundaries.

By actively managing how and when we engage with work, we create more space for personal fulfillment. This approach benefits our mental and physical health, strengthens our relationships, and enhances our job satisfaction. The journey to finding balance is ongoing and individual, yet universally essential. It requires us to regularly assess our priorities and make conscious adjustments to align our daily actions with our long-term goals for both career success and personal happiness.

SETTING BOUNDARIES FOR WORK-LIFE BALANCE

Drawing lines between work hours and personal time is like mapping out two distinct lands: one for our job duties and the other for our own happiness and health. This division goes beyond organizing our schedules. It's about honoring a key truth - that every side of our lives is important and deserves its own space, untouched by the other. To kickstart this journey, you could:

- Set clear start and finish times for your workday, sticking to them as consistently as you can.

- If your office is at home, fight the temptation to sneak a peek at emails or finish up tasks once those hours are up.

- Block out certain times or days exclusively for you or your family, marking these as no-work zones.

This approach isn't merely about having a timetable; it's fostering a culture of respect. Respect for our boundaries, for the preciousness of our personal time, and gaining respect from those we work alongside. These actions remind us that while our jobs are significant, they shouldn't take over our entire existence.

Yet, drawing these lines in theory and making sure they're followed are two different things. It demands open, honest talks with those we work with. It means being clear about when we're available and how critical it is to keep work and life balanced. To get your message across effectively, you might want to:

- Have real conversations with your bosses and teammates about needing time for both work and life.

- Politely decline extra tasks if they'd infringe on your personal time.

- Gently but firmly remind others of your limits if they forget.

It's crucial to understand that saying no isn't showing weakness; it's a sign of self-respect and standing by what matters to you. Regular communication can build a setting where your boundaries are seen and honored, reducing burnout risks and leading to a more balanced lifestyle.

Moreover, our environment plays a huge role in keeping our professional and home lives separate. With many of us working remotely nowadays, it's easy for these areas to blend. Creating specific spots in your home for work and for relaxation can greatly help maintain this separation. Here's how:

- Pick a spot for your work area, ideally away from where you relax or spend family time.

- Make sure places meant for relaxing are free from work stuff.

- Periodically check that your home arrangement supports your goal of balancing work and personal life.

These physical distinctions help our minds categorize our activities better, allowing us to switch more easily between work and leisure modes. It signals to our brain what we're supposed to focus on, depending on where we are, smoothing the transition between different parts of our day.

On a personal note, I found that when I used to take my laptop into the living room during family and grown-up evenings, it blurred the line between work and relaxation. Creating a dedicated workspace, where my notebook stays, has made a significant difference. It establishes a clear boundary and allows my brain to switch off from work more effectively, making my time with family truly relaxing.

Mental Switch Off: Rituals play a crucial role in mentally transitioning from work mode to personal time. One effective strategy is changing your environment or your attire at the end of your workday. For instance, swapping your work clothes for more casual attire can signal to your brain that the workday has ended. Similarly, moving from your home office to a different area can help delineate the boundary between professional and personal life. These simple actions set a physical and psychological marker, helping you leave work stress behind and fully engage with your personal life. It's much like the practices of historic figures such as Tchaikovsky and Edison, who used separate rooms to divide their creative pursuits and rest or other activities—illustrating even in their time the benefit of physically distinct spaces to enhance focus and relaxation.

Lastly, mastering the skills of delegating and prioritizing cannot be emphasized enough. Often, we take on too much in an attempt to prove ourselves or from fear of missing out. But biting off more than we can chew only brings stress and reduces how well we function in any aspect of our lives. To counter this, you can:

- List tasks that others can do, with clear guidelines and expected results.

- Pinpoint your top-priority tasks—those that matter most to your objectives—and give them your peak energy and hours.

- Keep checking that your commitments remain aligned with your priorities, tweaking as needed.

Through smart delegation, you lighten your own load and empower others by trusting them with tasks. By focusing on what's truly important, you ensure that your efforts are directed towards activities that genuinely benefit both your career and personal life, boosting your productivity and fulfillment.

It might be tough to delegate tasks, especially when striving for perfection. Yet, mastering this skill is invaluable. The focus shouldn't be on doing everything but on doing what matters most. Sorting tasks by necessity and impact, while shaking off the worry that things won't be perfect unless done personally, opens up more time for self-care, whether that's keeping fit, enjoying hobbies, or just taking a breather.

The symbiosis between our professional life and personal well-being is profound. Highlighted by recent research, individuals who maintain their boundaries enjoy higher job satisfaction and overall happiness (Harvard Business Review, 2022). This insight confirms the significant benefits that firm boundaries bring not just to our own lives but also to our efficiency and enthusiasm at work.

By adopting these habits, we unlock the real meaning of work-life balance. It goes beyond splitting hours evenly between job and joy; it's about enriching both aspects so they complement each other. When we honor our boundaries and communicate them clearly, we lay the groundwork for a life that's both satisfying and balanced.

EFFECTIVE TIME MANAGEMENT TECHNIQUES

Learning to manage your time efficiently is like getting better at playing a guitar. It takes dedication, regular practice, and that sprinkle of creativity. Whether it's juggling tasks at work or organizing our personal lives, wise time management can make our days both more productive and less hectic. This concept is a practical skill that we all can weave into our daily habits to boost our well-being.

Taking the first step towards effective time management means learning to tell apart which tasks are urgent and which ones are important. It's not only about jotting down everything on a piece of paper; it's about crafting a list that makes sense - one where tasks are sorted by their priority. This strategy shifts your focus to what really matters first, allowing you to allocate appropriate energy to high-priority tasks and schedule the rest for later. Here are some tips to get started:

- Kick off your day by pinpointing tasks that need immediate attention.

- Sort your tasks with the help of the urgent-important matrix.

- Dive into high-priority tasks right away before any distractions catch your eye.

- Keep revisiting and tweaking your priority list as your day unfolds.

Embracing this structured approach can turn a daunting list of to-dos into a clear and achievable set of goals, easing stress and curbing procrastination (P, n.d.).

Another key to mastering time management is making the most out of tools crafted to help us manage our schedules better. Be it the old-school pen and diary or trendy digital apps, there's no shortage of aids designed to keep us on track. For instance, time-blocking is an excellent way to divide your day into dedicated slots for specific tasks, reducing distractions and encouraging a mono-tasking mindset. To incorporate this into your daily planning:

- Pick a planner or app that feels right for you.

- Arrange your tasks in order of importance, assigning fixed times for concentrated effort.

- Don't forget to insert short breaks to stay fresh and maintain peak productivity.

- Make it a habit to assess how closely you're sticking to your plan and adjust as required.

Allocating distinct time slots for tasks using these tools can significantly curb the urge to flip between tasks unproductively.

Then, there's the trick of batching similar tasks, which simplifies your workflow and boosts your efficiency. By lumping together tasks of a kind, you avoid the mental strain of constantly switching contexts, enabling you to zoom in with greater focus. To put batching into action, consider:

- Grouping all your email checking and replying during certain times of the day.

- Placing all meetings or calls close together within a specific timeframe.

- Dedicating chunks of time for routine tasks, such as compiling reports or inputting data.
  Tailoring batching methods to suit how you work best can dramatically increase your productivity within the same time frame.

The Pomodoro Technique introduces a refreshing strategy for handling time better, working in focused spurts followed by brief pauses. This technique boosts concentration and ensures regular downtime to refresh, helping maintain a balanced pace throughout the day without burning out. Evaluating how we spend our time daily is crucial too, as it sheds light on potential areas for improvement. Knowing where our hours go allows us to consciously divert more time towards things that matter both personally and professionally.

Incorporating the Pomodoro Technique and daily reflections into your routine involves:

- Picking a task or a set of tasks.

- Setting a timer for 25 minutes to work without interruptions.

- Taking a 5-minute break when the timer rings, then starting another round.

- After completing four rounds, enjoy a longer break of 15-30 minutes.

- End your day with a short review of what you achieved and identify opportunities to enhance your time management.

If you prefer to try this technique with an app created for it, you can find many of them. Just search for Pomodoro, and you will find a great variety of Pomodoro Timer Apps.

PRIORITIZING SELF-CARE IN A BUSY SCHEDULE

In today's fast-paced world, where everything moves at the speed of light, taking a moment for ourselves often falls by the wayside. However, making self-care a part of our daily life isn't just nice to have; it's absolutely necessary for our overall health—both body and mind. It's time we start seeing self-care not as an optional indulgence but as a critical element of living a balanced life. This shift in perspective is key to keeping ourselves well in the midst of juggling work and personal commitments.

The convincing case for integrating self-care into our lives is clear when we consider its impact on our productivity and happiness. Simple pleasures like exercising, engaging in hobbies, or just giving ourselves time to unwind can greatly improve our quality of life. The question then becomes, "How do we make room for this?" Viewing self-care as essential as work meetings or project deadlines is the first step. By scheduling self-care activities deliberately, we acknowledge their significance and ensure they're a priority.

To weave self-care seamlessly into your schedule, try the following:

- Take a look at your current routine to spot times you might dedicate to nurturing yourself. Remember, even brief moments can be incredibly refreshing.

- Pick self-care activities that truly resonate with you and bring you peace, making them something you'll look forward to.

- Schedule these self-care moments ahead of time, giving them the same weight as any professional obligation.

Incorporating practices like mindfulness meditation, keeping a gratitude journal, or taking time for self-reflection can profoundly transform our relationship with ourselves. These practices help us forge a deeper connection with our inner selves, bringing emotional stability and resilience in turbulent times. Dedicating a few minutes each day to these practices can ground our days in tranquility and intention. Reflecting on how these moments enhance our mental clarity and ease stress underscores their immense value to our wellbeing.

Establishing boundaries is another vital aspect of making self-care a priority. Viewing self-care routines as mandatory meetings reserves specific times for our personal care, pushing back against the encroachment of professional pressures. Approaching self-care with kindness towards ourselves and recognizing the importance of indulging guilt-free in activities that nourish us can fend off burnout and bolster our resilience.

Here are some tips for setting those boundaries:

- Be open about your self-care schedule with coworkers and loved ones, highlighting its essential role in keeping you productive and healthy.

- Learn to decline extra tasks if they threaten to encroach upon your self-care time.

- Favor quality over quantity; even small acts of self-care can significantly boost your wellbeing.

By embedding self-care into our routines, we encourage consistency and embrace a comprehensive approach to wellness. Establishing calming morning rituals or relaxing evening routines can lay a foundation for a well-balanced existence. Acknowledging the benefits of self-care, from better focus to decreased stress, inspires us to keep up with these beneficial habits.

Cheryl Beutell, APRN, from Northwestern Medicine, supports this by saying, "a routine is how you build habits." She suggests that sticking to routines that promote better health can lead to a sense of calm and improved wellbeing (Staff, 2022).

Adapting to include self-care in our everyday routines doesn't have to be daunting. Begin with manageable steps, like dedicating a few minutes daily to meditation or journaling. These modest efforts can spark a significant transformation in our daily experiences, enriching both our personal and professional lives.

For Emily, a Sales Executive with a demanding job, integrating self-care into her daily routine is essential for maintaining her productivity and well-being.

Example Emily: Prioritizing Self-Care in a Busy Schedule

Morning Routine:

Emily starts her day with a short mindfulness meditation session, setting aside 10 minutes each morning to focus on her breath and center herself. This helps her approach the day's challenges with a calm and focused mind.

Work Boundaries:

To maintain a clear distinction between work and personal life, Emily sets specific work hours and adheres to them. She resists the temptation to check emails or finish up tasks once those hours are over.

Lunch Break:

Instead of working through lunch, Emily takes a 30-minute break to step outside and enjoy a walk. This provides her with a refreshing change of scenery and helps clear her mind.

Evening Ritual:

After a long day at work, Emily dedicates the first 30 minutes after arriving home to a self-care activity she loves, such as reading or practicing yoga. This time is reserved exclusively for her personal enjoyment.

Weekly Planning:

On Sundays, Emily spends an hour planning her week. She schedules self-care activities just as she would with work meetings or project deadlines, ensuring these moments are prioritized.

Delegation:

Emily practices delegating tasks at work to lighten her load. This allows her to focus on high-priority tasks and maintain a balanced workload.

By embedding self-care into her routine, Emily enhances her well-being and improves her productivity, demonstrating that self-care is essential for a successful and fulfilling life.

Creating a Supportive Work Environment

Building a supportive work environment is essential for balancing professional responsibilities with personal well-being. It starts with recognizing that coworkers are more than their roles; they are individuals with full lives beyond work. By cultivating an environment where open communication and trust flourish, we create a workplace where well-being and teamwork are prioritized.

Open dialogue is crucial—it involves setting up channels where feedback is actively sought and valued, concerns can be safely expressed, and everyone's achievements are celebrated as part of a team effort. Such an atmosphere not only makes work more satisfying but can also significantly reduce stress, shifting the focus from merely surviving to thriving.

Practical Steps to Cultivate a Supportive Atmosphere:

- **Encourage Communication:** Hold regular team meetings that invite everyone to share thoughts and concerns. Establish anonymous channels for staff to provide feedback, ensuring they can speak up without fear.

- **Celebrate Success:** Make it a point to publicly recognize both team and individual successes, showing appreciation for hard work and contributions.

When teamwork, empathy, and respect become everyday norms, morale and efficiency naturally improve. Feeling part of a caring community at work doesn't just enhance relationships—it strengthens the entire team. This emphasis on support transforms challenges into opportunities for growth and creativity, fostering a workplace where everyone feels acknowledged and valued.

Further Actions to Enhance Team Dynamics and Employee Well-being:

- **Organize Team-Building Events:** Plan activities that are not only fun but also build empathy and understanding.

- **Initiate Mentorship Programs:** Pair seasoned employees with new hires to create a welcoming and nurturing atmosphere.

- **Highlight Acts of Kindness:** Celebrate instances of

support among team members to promote a culture of empathy.

Embracing initiatives that promote work-life balance demonstrates a company's genuine concern for its employees' overall welfare. Offering flexible schedules, remote work options, and wellness programs are not just perks—they reflect the organization's commitment to treating staff as whole individuals with needs that extend beyond the office.

Implementing Work-Life Balance Measures:

- **Flexible Work Arrangements:** Provide options for flexible hours and telecommuting to help employees manage their personal and professional lives more effectively.

- **Wellness Programs:** Launch initiatives focused on physical and mental health, including access to counseling services and activities that promote health.

- **Regular Check-Ins:** Maintain ongoing communication with staff to understand their needs and preferences, using this feedback to continuously improve policies.

Furthermore, advocating for personal boundaries and self-care is crucial. It involves respecting personal time and the importance of unwinding. Encourage staff to set healthy limits without fear of missing out or repercussions for taking necessary breaks. Celebrating those who manage their commitments well sets a positive example and encourages everyone to prioritize their health, leading to a more balanced and enduring organizational culture.

Supporting Self-Care and Boundaries:

- **Establish Clear Guidelines:** Maintain firm policies that honor employees' downtime, ensuring they can truly disconnect.

- **Promote Self-Care Activities:** Support initiatives like meditation sessions or group workouts.

- **Recognize Healthy Practices:** Acknowledge and celebrate employees who maintain a healthy work-life balance, sharing their strategies and successes as inspiration for others.

By integrating these practices, companies can create an environment where employees feel truly valued and supported, leading to increased job satisfaction, loyalty, and a thriving workplace culture.

STRATEGIES FOR HARMONIZING PROFESSIONAL RESPONSIBILITIES WITH PERSONAL WELL-BEING

Throughout this chapter, we've navigated the complex yet rewarding task of juggling our career demands with the equally important aspects of self-care and personal happiness. Imagine tending to a garden; just as it blossoms under your care, your life too can bloom when you find that sweet spot between professional success and personal fulfillment.

Remember how we started this journey together? We emphasized the critical nature of drawing lines, organizing our days, putting ourselves first occasionally, and surrounding ourselves with a work environment that lifts us up rather than drags us down. These are practical steps essential for anyone wishing to lead a well-rounded life amidst the hustle and bustle of modern living.

As we gently pause here, at what feels like a rest stop on our ongoing adventure, it's crucial to understand that striving for balance is a continuous effort. This quest will manifest differently for each one of us, tailored by our distinct lives, dreams, and obstacles. While some advice may resonate more deeply with you, the underlying principle remains the same: cherish both your career and personal spaces.

Overlooking the significance of this equilibrium doesn't only affect us on a personal level - its waves are felt in our homes, workplaces, and communities, influencing overall contentment and efficiency. As you move beyond these pages, embrace the realization that harmonizing your professional and personal worlds is fundamental for a rich and satisfying existence.

SUMMARY

- **Understand the Challenge**: Recognize the daily conflict between professional duties and personal life, as seen in Laura's struggle to juggle work emails, family responsibilities, and self-care.1

- **Set Clear Boundaries**:

  - **Define Work Hours**: Firmly establish start and end times for your workday, respecting these limits to separate work from personal life, especially when working from home.

  - **Designate No-Work Zones**: Block out specific times for personal or family activities, ensuring these are strictly free from work interruptions.

- **Effective Communication**:

  - **Discuss Needs**: Have open conversations with employers and colleagues about balancing work and personal life needs.

  - **Advocate for Flexibility**: Negotiate for flexible working conditions that accommodate personal responsibilities.

- **Create Physical and Mental Separation**:

  - **Dedicated Workspaces**: Set up a specific area in your home for work tasks, distinct from areas reserved for relaxation.

  - **Mental Switch Off**: Use rituals like changing clothes or physical settings to transition between work and personal modes.

- **Prioritize and Delegate**:

  - **Prioritize Tasks**: Identify and focus on tasks that have the greatest impact on your goals, delegating or postponing less critical tasks.

  - **Empower Others**: Delegate tasks effectively to reduce personal workload, allowing focus on high-priority activities.

- **Incorporate Self-Care**:

  - **Schedule Self-Care Activities**: Treat self-care practices with the same importance as work meetings; schedule regular activities that promote well-being.

  - **Set Self-Care Boundaries**: Communicate your self-care times to others and respect these boundaries by avoiding work during these periods.

- **Cultivate a Supportive Work Environment**:

  - **Foster Open Communication**: Encourage a workplace culture that values open discussions about work-life balance.

  - **Promote Team Support**: Engage in team-building activities and mentorship programs that enhance understanding and support among colleagues.

- **Adopt Time Management Techniques**:

  - **Use Tools and Apps**: Leverage technology like planners and apps to organize and prioritize daily tasks effectively.

  - **Practice Time-Blocking**: Allocate specific time slots for different activities, reducing task-switching and enhancing focus.

- **Engage in Mindful Practices**:

  - **Mindfulness and Meditation**: Integrate mindfulness exercises like meditation or yoga to enhance focus and reduce stress.

  - **Reflective Practices**: End the day with reflection on achievements and areas for improvement in managing time and balancing activities.

CHAPTER FOUR

EMBRACING EMOTIONAL INTELLIGENCE

FOR HEALTHIER RELATIONSHIPS

What if I told you there's a hidden superpower lying dormant within you—one that could transform every relationship in your life? It's not a mystical force or ancient ritual, but something even more potent: emotional intelligence. With it, you gain the ability to truly understand those around you, to forge bonds that go beyond surface-level small talk. Emotional intelligence is the soul's secret language, allowing you to connect with others on a deeper, more meaningful plane. It's the catalyst for real empathy, for conversations that matter, for relationships that can weather any storm. Unlock this power, and you'll never view the world through the same lens again

In today's fast-paced world, it's easy to get caught up in a maze of miscommunications and misunderstandings. Relationships, which are meant to bring us closer, sometimes end up feeling like complicated puzzles. We trip, hesitate, and at times, fall, burdened by conflicts and confusions that appear insurmountable. At the core of many of these issues is a common challenge: the difficulty in both understanding and expressing our emotions clearly. Without even realizing it, we often hold back or misread emotions, erecting walls instead of building bridges. And this challenge isn't just confined to our personal lives; it stretches across all forms of interaction, leaving behind a string of missed opportunities to connect.

This chapter offers a beacon of hope, guiding us through the process of untangling these complex snarls. By diving into the significance of growing our self-awareness and self-regulation, improving our empathy, and honing our active listening abilities, we're encouraged to embark on a path toward healthier, more resilient relationships. Through straightforward, actionable steps, we'll learn how paying attention to our own emotions and tuning into the feelings of others can pave the way for greater mutual understanding and connection. This endeavor goes beyond merely dodging disagreements; it's about creating an atmosphere where every talk helps us become closer friends, and every time we understand each other, it helps us build lasting friendships based on trust and respect.

By engaging with emotional intelligence, we equip ourselves with the tools needed not only to navigate but also to enhance our interactions at every turn. This heightened awareness allows us to be more present and responsive, making it easier to understand where others are coming from and communicate in ways that resonate more deeply. The journey towards integrating emotional intelligence into our daily lives might initially seem daunting, yet, with patience and practice, the rewards it brings to our relationships are immense and profoundly impactful.

As we explore emotional intelligence further, we'll discover it's about more than just managing emotions—it enriches every aspect of how we relate. From recognizing the subtle cues in body language to appreciating the power of a kindly word, emotional intelligence nurtures a sense of communion and understanding that transcends the ordinary. It encourages us to look beyond the surface, to connect not just with our eyes but with our hearts. Emotional intelligence fosters an environment where compassion and meaningful connection can truly flourish.

This exploration of emotional intelligence is a practical guide to living a more connected and empathetic life. Whether it's navigating the complexities of family dynamics, enhancing workplace relationships, or deepening bonds with friends, the principles outlined here hold the key to unlocking richer, more fulfilling interactions. By committing to this journey, we open ourselves up to the possibility of transforming every encounter into an opportunity for growth and connection.

DEVELOPING SELF-AWARENESS AND SELF-REGULATION

Maintaining meaningful connections with people is deeply rooted in our ability to understand and manage our emotions. It's about improving how we handle our feelings to enrich and enhance our interactions with others. When we grasp what we're feeling, we can see how it affects those around us, especially the ones closest to our hearts.

Understanding our emotions as they happen marks the beginning of emotional intelligence. It's about catching ourselves in the moment of feeling something and recognizing how these feelings steer our thoughts and actions. This insight is vital because it sets the stage for empathy—putting ourselves in someone else's shoes, thanks to our own experiences. However, reaching this awareness level doesn't just happen; it takes deliberate effort. As we explored in detail in Chapter 2, mindfulness is a powerful tool for enhancing self-awareness. It teaches us to observe our thoughts and feelings without judgment. Building on the foundations set in that chapter, here are some straightforward steps to enhance your mindfulness practice:

- Spend a few minutes daily sitting quietly, tuning into your breath.

- As you get used to this exercise, start acknowledging your emotions and silently naming them.

- Think about how these emotions affect your response to various events.

Then, there's self-regulation, which kicks in once we're mindful of our emotions. This skill helps us handle our feelings and urges so they don't overrun us. Effectively regulating our emotions involves staying calm during stressful times, communicating appropriately, and avoiding impulsive reactions that could harm our relationships. Techniques like deep breathing and positive self-talk can be powerful allies in navigating tough emotions. Try these methods:

- Counteract negative thoughts or fears with encouraging affirmations.

- Find constructive ways to share your feelings, possibly by confiding in a trusted friend.

- In moments of stress, breathe slowly and deeply to quiet your mind. Refer to the techniques outlined in Chapter 2 for guidance.

Enhancing emotional intelligence skills, particularly those related to relationship management, can significantly improve how we interact and connect with others. Relationship management involves building a bond over time by integrating other emotional intelligence skills like self-awareness, self-management, and social awareness. This comprehensive approach allows us to maintain healthy relationships by understanding our own emotions and those of others, expressing our feelings constructively, and effectively managing interactions, even during stressful times (Bradberry and Greaves, 2009).

For example, you can improve your relationship management skills by remaining curious about your partner's thoughts and feelings, asking open-ended questions to deepen your understanding. Validating their emotions, even when you disagree, shows respect and acknowledgment of their perspective. Additionally, using humor and other repair attempts can prevent conflicts from escalating, while focusing on creating positive experiences can strengthen the bond.

Let's pause the theory for a moment and jump into a little story to see these ideas in action. Imagine if our relationship tips were characters in a sitcom. In today's episode, we meet Olivia and Tom, a couple who could really use a laugh—and maybe a new strategy or two to tackle their household chores. Let's see how a little emotional intelligence turns their chore war into a chore... less war-like situation.

Olivia and Tom often found themselves in a stand-off over who should do the dishes after dinner. One evening, instead of the usual standoff, Olivia decided to try something different. She approached Tom with genuine curiosity, asking, 'What's making it hard for you to help with the dishes?' This wasn't an accusation but a sincere question. Tom, taken aback by her tone, opened up about his overwhelming project deadlines at work.

They both laughed when Olivia joked about Tom's well-known distaste for the smell of dish soap, which lightened the mood. She then playfully suggested a 'dishwashing dance-off' to make the mundane task more enjoyable. Tom agreed, and they ended up having a fun time cleaning together, which not only got the dishes done but also brought them closer.

These shared moments of levity not only enrich our daily interactions but also enable us to handle life's challenges with a smile, finding joy and growth in the everyday.

At the same time, it's important to address other crucial aspects such as drawing personal boundaries and engaging in self-care. Establishing boundaries allows us to define our comfort levels and expectations, essential for mutual respect and understanding. Self-care ensures that we are emotionally and physically prepared to engage positively in our relationships.

To weave these practices into your life, consider:

- Speaking up about your needs and boundaries with friends or your partner.

- Making time for activities that refresh you mentally and physically.

- Kindly but firmly maintaining your boundaries when they're tested.

ENHANCING EMPATHY AND ACTIVE LISTENING SKILLS

As we explored in Chapter 2, active listening is a crucial component of mindful communication, allowing us to be fully present and engaged in our interactions with others. By paying close attention to both verbal and non-verbal cues and responding with empathy and understanding, we can foster deeper, more meaningful connections and enhance our overall well-being.

In this chapter, we'll build upon the concept of active listening and explore how it plays a vital role in developing emotional intelligence and nurturing healthier relationships. While the core principles of active listening remain the same, we'll delve into how this skill can be applied to better understand and validate others' emotions, perspectives, and needs.

By honing our active listening skills in the context of emotional intelligence, we can improve our ability to navigate conflicts, provide support, and strengthen our interpersonal relationships. Through practical exercises and real-life examples, we'll discover how active listening forms the foundation of empathy and effective communication, enabling us to build trust, foster understanding, and create more harmonious connections with those around us.

As we continue our journey towards personal growth and well-being, it's essential to recognize how the skills and strategies we've discussed throughout this book are interconnected and mutually reinforcing. By applying active listening in both mindful communication and emotionally intelligent interactions, we can cultivate a more compassionate, understanding, and fulfilling approach to our relationships and daily life. As we delve into the practical applications of active listening in building emotional intelligence and stronger relationships, we'll first explore the crucial role of empathy in fostering deeper connections.

Empathy, or the ability to understand and share the feelings of others, plays a crucial role in building deep and meaningful relationships. By actively listening during our daily conversations, we can strengthen this skill. Active listening is more than just hearing words; it involves fully engaging with the speaker by giving them your undivided attention and acknowledging their emotions and viewpoints. This kind of engagement paves the way for greater understanding, allowing trust and closeness to develop.

To become an effective active listener, consider these simple yet powerful steps:

- Commit to paying full attention to the speaker, eliminating any distractions.

- Show that you're involved in the conversation through nonverbal signals like nodding or maintaining eye contact.

- Acknowledge the speaker's feelings with affirming statements. Saying something like, 'That sounds really challenging,' can convey your empathy and understanding, making the conversation feel more connected and sincere.

- Rather than jumping to conclusions, ask questions to clarify their points.

Empathetic communication is about both understanding and feeling the emotions of others, laying the groundwork for trust and connection in our relationships (Active Listening and Empathy for Human Connection, n.d.). When individuals feel truly heard and valued, they are more inclined to open up, deepening the emotional bond and fostering mutual respect. Though it may seem straightforward, mastering empathetic communication takes conscious effort and practice, but the rewards—enhanced interactions and stronger bonds—are well worth it.

Active listening goes beyond merely acknowledging what someone says verbally. It includes reading nonverbal cues, mirroring emotions, and seeking further clarification. Picture yourself attentively listening to a friend discussing a concern; by echoing their feelings ("It seems like you're quite stressed about this.") and asking insightful questions ("What do you think caused this situation?"), you demonstrate true interest in their experience. This not only helps you grasp the issue more clearly but also solidifies your emotional connection.

Improving our empathy and active listening skills can greatly increase our emotional intelligence, enabling us to build more meaningful and satisfying connections. Emotional intelligence, the ability to comprehend and manage our emotions as well as recognize and influence others', is vital for all kinds of relationships, personal and professional alike. By enhancing our emotional intelligence through empathy and active listening, we lay the foundation for relationships based on understanding and respect.

Cultivating these skills does more than foster personal development; it has tangible benefits in our day-to-day lives. Strong emotional ties lead to smoother interactions, whether at home, work, or within our communities, creating spaces where everyone feels heard, understood, and appreciated. Such environments are essential for fostering collaborative and supportive relationships.

However, it's crucial to understand that developing these abilities requires time, patience, and genuine effort to improve how we connect with those around us. Offering someone your complete attention in today's distraction-filled world sends a strong message of caring and respect.

By embracing the journey to become better listeners and more empathetic individuals, we'll see our relationships flourish. At the core of this endeavor lies a sincere wish to authentically connect with others. Making these skills a priority not only improves our own lives but also contributes to a kinder, more connected world.

Practical Exercise:
Active Listening Practice

- Engage in a conversation with a friend, family member, or colleague, focusing on practicing active listening skills.

- Give the speaker your undivided attention, maintaining eye contact and showing interest through nonverbal cues like nodding.

- Paraphrase what the speaker has said to ensure understanding, and ask clarifying questions when necessary.

- Reflect on how actively listening and showing empathy impacted the quality and depth of the conversation.

RESOLVING CONFLICTS THROUGH EMOTIONAL UNDERSTANDING

Emotional intelligence is a hidden gem in the realm of resolving disputes. It allows us to convey our feelings calmly and use "I" statements effectively, keeping the spotlight on understanding rather than pointing fingers. By embracing emotional intelligence, we unlock the ability to unravel what really lies beneath a conflict, setting the stage for a resolution based on mutual understanding.

Here are some communication ideas worth trying:

- Begin by sharing your feelings with "I" statements to take responsibility for your emotions instead of casting blame.

- Stay calm and aim to grasp the emotions that fuel the other person's point of view.

- Give your full attention to the concerns others voice, recognizing their sentiments without rushing to judge or offer fixes.

Examples:

1. Imagine a scenario where Sophia feels overlooked at work because her team often holds meetings at a time when she's picking up her children from school. Using emo-

tional intelligence, she approaches her manager and says, "I feel left out of important decisions because I'm not available at the current meeting time. Can we explore alternative timings so I can contribute more effectively?" By using "I" statements, Sarah takes responsibility for her feelings without blaming her team, opening up a constructive dialogue focused on finding a solution.

2. Consider Noah and Alex who are roommates clashing over household chores. Noah decides to use his emotional intelligence skills by saying, "I feel frustrated when the living room is messy because I need a clean space to relax after work. How do you feel about it?" This approach keeps the conversation calm and centered on understanding each other's perspectives rather than accusing Alex of not cleaning.

This strategy reduces the likelihood of defensive reactions and fosters an environment where everyone feels seen and respected. By striving to view the situation from the other person's vantage point, we embark on an exercise of perspective-taking that not only enhances our comprehension but also fosters empathy. This empathic approach clears up misunderstandings and strengthens our connections, laying the groundwork for meaningful conversations. To get better at empathy, you might want to:

- Make a deliberate effort to set your own views aside for a moment and truly consider others' perspectives.

- Pose open-ended questions to delve into their emotions and thoughts, showing real interest and care.

- Paraphrase their points of view to confirm your understanding and show you're actively listening.

Example: Jane and Mark's Workplace Conflict Resolution

Imagine a situation in a corporate setting where two team members, Jane and Mark, disagree on the direction of a project. Jane believes the project should prioritize speed to market, while Mark feels more thorough testing is necessary to ensure product quality. Initially, their discussions are tense, and both are somewhat defensive, feeling that their professional judgment is being questioned.

To address this, their manager employs the strategy of empathy and perspective-taking:

1. The manager begins by asking Jane and Mark to set aside their initial positions and consider the broader goals of the company (Setting Aside Personal Views)

2. The manager asks open-ended questions like, "Jane, what are your main concerns about delaying the project launch?" and "Mark, can you explain why you believe additional testing is crucial?" (Open-Ended Questions)

3. After they respond, the manager paraphrases their points, saying, "So, Jane, your priority is to capture market share quickly, while Mark, you are focused on long-term customer satisfaction through product reliability." (Paraphrasing for Understanding)

Through this process, Jane and Mark start to see each other's perspectives more clearly. They recognize that both speed and quality are essential, leading them to collaborate on a solution that schedules phased testing alongside preliminary market release preparations.

By actively listening and encouraging empathy, the manager not only defuses the potential for conflict but also helps foster a collaborative solution that respects both team members' contributions. This approach not only clears up misunderstandings but also strengthens their professional relationship, laying the groundwork for more effective teamwork in the future.

This example shows how understanding and empathic communication can turn a potentially divisive situation into an opportunity for collaboration and mutual understanding.

Moreover, being clear about our emotions and practicing active listening are fundamental to communicating effectively. Good communication goes beyond simple word exchanges; it means connecting with the heart of what's being shared on an emotional level. By adopting these methods, we ensure fewer misunderstandings and a smoother path to finding solutions:

- When you talk about your feelings, be precise about what you're feeling and why.

- Engage in active listening by fully focusing on the speaker, acknowledging through nods, and rephrasing their words to check your understanding.

- Give your full attention by not interrupting or planning your response while the other person is speaking. This approach not only shows respect but also deepens your understanding of the conversation.

These methods, as highlighted by McCarthy (n.d.), showcase how crucial emotional intelligence is in navigating and resolving conflicts efficiently.

Addressing conflicts with emotional understanding and empathy leads to more than just settlement; it paves the way for productive discussions and mutual compromises. By approaching issues with empathy and emotional awareness, we give priority to the relationship over the disagreement itself. Though it doesn't call for a checklist-like method, adopting this attitude builds healthier, stronger connections. It turns conflict from a divider into a chance for growth and deeper understanding among all involved. Constructive dialogue based on empathy isn't about winning; it's about enriching relationships in ways that are beneficial for everyone.

The role of emotional intelligence in conflict resolution is immeasurable. It changes the dynamic from confrontational to cooperative, seeking solutions that work for everyone involved. People who possess high emotional intelligence consistently find resolutions that cater to the needs and interests of each party, underlining emotional intelligence's role in reaching compromises (Jordan & Troth; MSU Extension, n.d.).

In summary, nurturing and applying emotional intelligence in our dealings, especially during conflicts, guides us toward broader mutual respect, understanding, and eventually, reconciliation. This entails recognizing conflicts as opportunities to strengthen ties and alliances, provided we tackle them with the right mindset—empathy, effective communication, and emotional insight. As we manage our relationships, be they personal or professional, leaning on these principles of emotional intelligence prepares us to address disagreements constructively, transforming potential discord into chances for growth and closeness.

NURTURING HEALTHY RELATIONSHIPS THROUGH EMOTIONAL INTELLIGENCE

Boosting emotional intelligence (EQ) is crucial for building strong, resilient relationships. It's about realizing that emotional connection is not just a bonus but is essential for flourishing together. By being empathetic, understanding, and communicating effectively, we can manage the intricate aspects of our relationships with more ease and contentment.

At its core, empathy plays a vital role. Being able to understand and share someone else's feelings helps us connect on a much deeper level with those we care about. It involves seeing things from their point of view, validating their emotions, and responding with kindness. While not everyone might find this easy at first, the wonderful thing about EQ is that it can grow stronger with time.

The transformative potential of emotional intelligence in relationships is beautifully illustrated by a personal story from my own life. When I transitioned to my second university, I encountered a communication style among the students that was remarkably different from anything I had experienced before. The students there frequently asked questions and made requests, but they did so with a friendly, considerate manner that I found striking.

In this new environment, I observed how their approach to communication fostered a sense of openness, respect, and collaboration. The students showed genuine interest in each other's perspectives and were unafraid to seek clarification or assistance when needed. This created an atmosphere where everyone felt heard, valued, and supported.

Inspired by this experience, I began to incorporate this communication style into my own life. I made a conscious effort to ask questions with curiosity and kindness, and to make requests with a friendly, respectful tone. Over time, this new approach became second nature to me, transforming the way I interacted with others.

The impact of this change extended far beyond my personal life. Years later, I found myself naturally employing this communication style within my own family. By modeling this approach, I witnessed a profound shift in our family dynamics. Our interactions became more positive, open, and supportive. We were better able to understand each other's needs and perspectives, leading to stronger, more harmonious relationships. This shows the ripple effect that the little community at my second university had on myself and my family, and it might continue to spread even further.

It's important to note that in my family, like in all families, we occasionally face challenges. However, by consistently applying the principles of emotionally intelligent communication, we are better equipped to navigate these situations with empathy, understanding, and respect.

This experience taught me the incredible power of emotional intelligence in action. By adopting a communication style rooted in empathy, respect, and kindness, we can create ripple effects that extend far beyond our immediate interactions. When we nurture emotionally intelligent communication, we not only enrich our own relationships but also contribute to a more compassionate and connected world.

As we continue on our journey to cultivate emotional intelligence, let us remember the transformative potential of even small changes in our communication patterns. By embracing a more empathetic, considerate approach, we open the door to deeper understanding, stronger connections, and more fulfilling relationships in all aspects of our lives.

Trust, intimacy, and resilience are fundamental qualities nurtured by focusing on emotional connections and support. Trust acts as the bedrock for any healthy relationship, built through consistent actions and decisions that show we are reliable, respectful, and dedicated. Intimacy stems from being open and vulnerable, which, although scary, strengthens bonds like nothing else. It's about letting each other in, imperfections and all, and embracing each other completely. Resilience means facing ups and downs together without falling apart, choosing to tackle problems as a team rather than allowing them to push you apart.

For a relationship to truly thrive, it needs emotional honesty, openness, and mutual respect. These elements create a safe space where both people feel appreciated for their true selves. Authenticity leads to a transparent environment free from pretense. Vulnerability, often mistaken for weakness, is actually a superpower in relationships, inviting greater closeness. Respect ensures that personal boundaries are acknowledged and honored. Keeping these qualities alive, especially during conflict, is challenging but pivotal for maintaining a healthy dynamic.

By enhancing our emotional intelligence, we're not just enriching our relationships but also our overall well-being and happiness, alongside ensuring these bonds last (Bisignano, 2018). Working on our EQ allows us to experience contentment, feel capable, and maintain a positive outlook on our relationships. When both partners feel listened to, understood, and valued, satisfaction is naturally high. Longevity follows from continually cultivating these aspects, forging a connection resilient enough to stand the test of time.

One of the most rewarding parts of developing EQ in relationships is how it transcends the partnership, fostering personal growth and positively affecting those around us. It teaches us patience, empathy, and compassion, making us better listeners and more mindful individuals. This, in turn, enriches our interactions with friends, family, and colleagues, contributing to a more empathetic community.

However, attaining such a level of emotional intelligence takes conscious effort. It requires regular introspection, an eagerness to learn and evolve, and the humility to accept our faults. Open and honest communication, active listening, and tackling disagreements constructively are all part of the journey. Though challenging, the payoff—a deeply fulfilling, loving, and supportive relationship—is incredibly rewarding.

THE TRANSFORMATIVE POWER OF EMOTIONAL INTELLIGENCE IN RELATIONSHIPS

Throughout our exploration in this chapter, we've embarked on a journey through the world of emotional intelligence (EQ) and witnessed its incredible power to foster deeper and more meaningful connections. Initially, we touched upon how understanding ourselves and managing our emotions pave the way for stronger bonds with others. Looking back, it's evident that at the heart of EQ—whether it involves empathy, active listening, resolving conflicts, or building supportive relationships—is a genuine effort to appreciate and acknowledge both our feelings and those of the people in our lives.

Adopting emotional intelligence is crucial for anyone aiming to deepen their relationships and enhance their quality of life. It doesn't matter if you're a teenager experiencing the complexities of new relationships or an adult working through longstanding ones; the principles of EQ are universally beneficial, leading to more fulfilling and durable connections.

SUMMARY

- **Key Concept**: Emotional intelligence (EQ) is an essential skill that deepens our comprehension, empathy, and connection with others. It transcends simple emotion management, enriching every interaction and strengthening relationships across all areas of life.

- **Challenges in Relationships**: Common issues like miscommunications and misunderstandings often stem from poor use of emotional intelligence. Enhancing EQ can help overcome these barriers and lead to more fulfilling relationships.

- **Benefits of Emotional Intelligence**:

  - **Improved Self-awareness**: Recognizing and understanding one's own emotions can lead to better control and expression, enhancing interactions with others.

  - **Better Conflict Resolution**: Using emotional intelligence in conflicts can transform disputes into opportunities for growth and understanding.

- **Deeper Empathy and Listening**: Active listening and empathy are critical for building trust and understanding, essential for strong relationships.

- **Practical Steps to Enhance EQ**:

  - **Mindfulness and Self-regulation**: Techniques such as mindfulness meditation help enhance awareness of one's emotions and how they influence behavior.

  - **Active Listening**: Engaging fully in conversations and showing genuine interest in others' feelings and thoughts.

  - **Managing Emotions in Conflicts**: Using techniques to stay calm and communicate effectively during disagreements.

- **Cultivating EQ in Daily Life**:

  - **Mindful Communication**: Paying attention to non-verbal cues and being present in conversations.

  - **Empathy in Action**: Practicing empathy by trying to understand and share the feelings of others, enhancing personal and professional relationships.

- **Long-term Benefits**:

  - **Strengthened Personal and Professional Relationships**: Higher emotional intelligence leads to improved communication and understanding, fostering stronger bonds.

- **Increased Personal Well-being**: Better handling of emotional challenges contributes to overall happiness and satisfaction in life.

- **Call to Action**:

  - Incorporate EQ-enhancing practices like mindfulness and active listening into daily routines.

  - Remain open to continuous learning and improvement in emotional intelligence skills.

Chapter Five

Finding Joy Through Gratitude and Positivity

In our whirlwind lives, where the days and nights blur together and fleeting moments vanish before we can grasp them, it's all too easy to lose sight of the sweet bliss that gratitude and a positive outlook bring. Caught up in the hustle and seeking endlessly for more, we often miss out on savoring the riches that already make our existence meaningful. It's like we're on a never-ending search for happiness in far-off places, not realizing that real treasure is hidden within our day-to-day life.

This oversight, however, comes with its price. Neglecting gratitude and positivity doesn't just rob us of the chance to enjoy life's delights but also leaves us in a state of constant craving, always reaching for happiness that just slips away. But it goes beyond just missing out on joy; it concerns the impact this scarcity has on our overall sense of well-being. Overlooking the positives in our lives is like wandering through a foggy landscape, where the beauty of the surroundings is obscured by a veil of dissatisfaction. This constant search for something better can blind us to the value of the experiences and relationships that enrich our lives profoundly.

Understanding this, the conversation shifts to hands-on ways to cultivate deep-rooted gratitude and an unshakeably positive attitude. By weaving simple habits like keeping a gratitude journal, practicing mindful appreciation, and performing small acts of kindness into our daily life, we unlock the potential for a personal transformation. This path involves adopting subtle yet powerful changes that guide us toward peace, meaningful connections, and genuine joy in our daily lives. Through these deliberate steps, we set off toward a fuller life, lit by the glow of gratitude and positivity, ushering in a realm where contentment flourishes even in the most ordinary moments.

BUILDING A GRATITUDE PRACTICE

Bringing a sense of gratitude into your day enriches your life, and it's not just a feel-good idea—it's backed by science as a proven way to enhance happiness and overall well-being. Making the effort to recognize and appreciate the good things happening around you every day does wonders for lifting your spirits and building a foundation for a happier life. Let's explore some straightforward but powerful ways to develop a mindset filled with gratitude.

Kicking off with a gratitude journal is an incredible method to help turn your attention to the positive moments in life. Health experts stand behind this practice, pointing to its numerous benefits for both mental and physical well-being. The idea is simple yet profound. Every day, carve out a little time to write down three things you're thankful for. These can be big achievements or tiny joys—the importance lies in acknowledging and valuing them. Doing this regularly trains your brain to spot more of the good stuff in your surroundings, leading to an uplift in your general happiness.

Here are a few steps to get started with your gratitude journaling:

- Pick a special notebook or digital app where you'll keep your gratitude notes.

- Every day, write down three experiences or things that made you smile or that you're grateful for.

- Take a moment to think about why these particular things meant so much to you.

Saying "thank you" to people not only makes your day brighter but lights up theirs too, spreading a wave of positive vibes. A heartfelt word of thanks, whether through a message, face-to-face conversation, or a small deed, reinforces your connections and blankets your circle with warmth and kindness.

To weave gratitude into your interactions:

- Each week, think of at least one person you feel thankful towards and plan how you can express your gratitude.

- It could be through a thoughtful note or a sincere verbal thank you, focusing on what you genuinely appreciate about them.

- Turn this into a regular practice and watch the wonderful effect it has on your relationships.

Diving deep into mindful gratitude practices enables you to fully embrace and cherish the present blessings. Being truly in the moment and valuing what we have right now—like the natural beauty around us, the comfort of our homes, or time spent with loved ones—amplifies our ability to treasure these aspects of our lives.

To practice mindfulness in gratitude:

- Set aside time each day for quiet reflection on what brings you joy and contentment.

- Try mindfulness or meditation focused on gratitude, allowing yourself to sink deeply into feelings of thankfulness.

Making gratitude a staple in your daily rituals ensures that this sense of thankfulness remains a vibrant part of your everyday existence. Slight tweaks to your routine can act as gentle nudges to stop for a moment and appreciate the richness of your life. This habit boosts mindfulness and at the same time keeps the spirit of gratitude alive throughout your day.

Ideas for integrating gratitude into daily habits include:

- Adding a gratitude moment to your morning or evening routines, reflecting on the day's gifts or looking forward to tomorrow's promises.

- Using daily signals like meal times or a stroll as reminders to consider something you're grateful for.

The impact of consistent gratitude exercises is remarkable, with studies showing they can indeed change the brain to spotlight more positive experiences. By adopting a gratitude practice, you're enhancing your own joy and well-being, while also contributing to making the world a kinder, more grateful place.

CULTIVATING A POSITIVE MINDSET

Embracing a positive mindset transcends the typical advice found in self-help literature; it embodies a powerful tool, affirmed by psychological research, to stay optimistic and resilient amidst life's hurdles. Visualize trekking through existence with a guide that solely points to gloom and desolation. In such scenarios, spotting even a flicker of hope becomes a Herculean task.

One effective technique for nurturing a positive mindset is cultivating positive self-talk. This involves regularly repeating straightforward yet potent phrases that can spark a shift in how we view life. For example, rather than dwelling on feelings of inadequacy, positive self-talk propels us towards recognizing our strengths and possibilities.

Here's a gentle nudge on how to weave this practice into the fabric of our daily lives:

- Kick off your day by voicing three positive statements about yourself or your abilities.

- Faced with a tough situation? Take a moment to ponder alternative, positive interpretations.

- Counteract pessimistic self-dialogue with affirmations

that spotlight your capabilities.

In my own experience, I found this practice to be incredibly effective. There was a time in my life when my inner voice frequently said, "I am so exhausted" during breaks. Using this technique, I changed my affirmation to "What do I do next?" This short phrase helped me think about stepping forward positively into my day. Listen to your mind and identify those negative repetitive sentences, then think about a positive sentence to replace them. For me, this change brought more energy and positivity.

The environment we immerse ourselves in plays a crucial role in nurturing a positive mindset. The content we consume and the people we surround ourselves with deeply influence our perspective. Immersing ourselves in encouraging books, uplifting tunes, or empowering podcasts feeds our mind with optimism.

Putting joy and self-care at the forefront is like laying down a resilient foundation for a home designed to weather any storm. It means acknowledging and attending to our needs - be they physical, emotional, or spiritual. Delving into activities that light up our world, embracing mindfulness, and practicing self-compassion form the cornerstone of this approach. Here are some gentle suggestions:

- Allocate time each week for activities that recharge your soul.

- Cultivate a mindfulness practice, which could be meditation, yoga, or quiet moments in nature, facilitating a deeper connection with oneself.

Performing acts of kindness creates a symbiotic relationship between our happiness and the well-being of others. The true beauty of these actions lies in their mutual benefit: they uplift both the doer and the recipient. Whether through volunteering, lending a hand to a neighbor, or merely sharing a smile with someone we pass by, these gestures knit a fabric of positivity and community connection. Participating in kind deeds fills us with a sense of fulfillment and belonging, making our hearts swell with joy.

One of my most cherished birthdays was spent thousands of miles away from home in a small beach town where I knew no one. I wandered into a quaint photography shop and admired the beautiful portraits adorning the walls. At that time, I was deeply passionate about landscape photography. The photographer and I struck up a conversation, and she shared how fulfilling it was to capture people and their expressions. Her words resonated with me, and as I left the shop, I felt an overwhelming sense of happiness. I must have had a huge smile on my face because everyone I passed mirrored my joy with their own bright smiles. It was a profound realization that happiness is contagious and can be shared with others effortlessly. That birthday, marked by this beautiful exchange of smiles, remains one of my happiest memories.

A solid pledge to adopt a positive mindset does wonders beyond improving everyday experiences; it arms us with the resilience needed to gracefully dance through the ebbs and flows of life. Studies such as those by the Mayo Clinic (Mayo Clinic, 2023) reveal that an optimistic outlook can lead to better physical health, reduced stress, and even a longer, more blissful existence. This intricate connection between positive thinking and tangible health benefits highlights the significant effect our mindset has on our life's quality and overall wellness.

EMBRACING OPTIMISM DURING CHALLENGES

Learning to stay positive even when things get tough builds strong foundations that help us handle anything life throws at us. The key is to view every challenge as an opportunity to grow. Enjoying activities that reduce stress, leaning on friends and family for support, and setting realistic goals are practical steps to fill our lives with joy and strength.

Let's talk about seeing hurdles as growth opportunities. This viewpoint demands a significant shift in how we think, steering clear from the doom-and-gloom mindset that paints every problem as a colossal barrier. By adjusting our lens, we recognize these trials as moments ripe for learning, evolving, and strengthening. Here's a simple guide on how to make this shift:

- When facing a setback, pause, breathe deeply, like you have learned in Chapter 2.

- Ponder over what this hiccup can teach you.

- Visualize how conquering this obstacle will empower you, enhancing your wisdom or fortitude.

This approach doesn't just help us manage difficulties; it instills a sense of purpose during tough times and fosters our ability to adapt and improve.

Integrating Mindfulness and Social Support

When it comes to melting away stress, yoga and meditation have emerged as more than just passing fads - and for good reason. Both promote mindfulness, an engaged awareness of our current state, helping us accept our emotions, thoughts, and bodily feelings. This acceptance lowers stress and fosters peace. If you're curious but haven't dipped your toes in yet, why not start simple?

- Allocate five minutes daily for meditation or some gentle yoga.

- During these sessions, let your breath center your thoughts, gently corralling them back when they wander off.

- A helpful technique is to count each exhalation, starting from 20 and counting down to 1, then repeating the cycle. This method keeps your mind focused and prevents it from wandering.

These practices act like a soft reset for your nervous system, offering clarity and tranquility amidst life's storms.

The role of social support in our lives is monumental. In those rough patches, the encouragement and outlook we gain from our relationships are priceless. Cultivating these connections before trouble strikes means we've got a robust network ready to prop us up when needed. Strengthening these ties can be straightforward:

- Ensure regular catch-ups with loved ones, be it through messages or calls.

- Don't hold back on sharing your battles; letting others in to help only strengthens your bond.

Social circles provide us with a comforting shoulder and practical aid, serving as a reminder that we're not alone in our fight. This aspect is invaluable for our resilience, offering both perspective and strength during hard times.

Setting and Celebrating Goals

Setting realistic goals and recognizing every achievement helps maintain resilience. To make this work:

- Break big dreams into smaller, more approachable tasks.

- Applaud yourself for every step forward, valuing your dedication and strides made.

This practice keeps us motivated and reaffirms our ability to progress through challenges.

Optimism is more than hoping for the best; it's about actively using our skills and insights to navigate life's challenges. It's understanding, as noted by Miller (2021), that resilience involves using our experiences and even our trials as catalysts for growth and progress.

Real-Life Example:
Maria's Journey Through Adversity

Maria runs a local cafe, which was hit hard during an economic downturn. Initially overwhelmed with worries about the future of her business, Maria decided to view the situation not as an insurmountable setback but as a chance to evolve and adapt. She started by taking small steps to reduce stress and revitalize her business model.

1. **Mindful Adaptation:**
   o Maria began practicing yoga each morning before opening the cafe. These sessions helped her maintain calm and stay focused throughout the day.
   o She also used this time to reflect on her business, leading her to innovate a delivery service that catered to her community's growing need for contactless options.

2. **Leveraging Social Support:**
   o Recognizing the importance of community, Maria reached out to fellow local business owners to form a support network. They shared resources, like bulk buying supplies to reduce costs, and promoted each other's businesses through social media.
   o She kept her employees engaged and motivated by regularly checking in and being transparent about the business's challenges and what steps were being taken to overcome them.

3. Setting New Goals:

o Maria set realistic weekly goals for her business, celebrating small victories with her team, such as the successful launch of a new menu item or a positive customer review.

o These celebrations kept morale high and reinforced her team's commitment to the cafe's success.

Through these strategies, Maria not only managed to keep her cafe afloat but also strengthened her ties with her community and employees. Her story is a testament to how adopting a mindset of growth and resilience, and integrating mindfulness and social support, can transform challenges into opportunities for development and fulfillment.

Maria's example illustrates that optimism isn't merely about hoping for the best but actively engaging with challenges using personal and communal resources. This proactive approach to life's difficulties highlights the importance of resilience and the powerful role it plays in personal and professional success.

DEEPENING CONNECTIONS
THROUGH APPRECIATION

After exploring how gratitude and a positive mindset empower us to handle life's challenges and enhance our well-being, it's important to focus on a specific aspect of gratitude that profoundly affects our relationships: appreciation. Appreciation isn't just about feeling thankful; it's about actively expressing this gratitude to deepen connections and reinforce the bonds we share with others. This active engagement can transform our interactions and significantly boost the collective morale and emotional resilience of our communities.

Cultivating Appreciation in Everyday Interactions

Appreciation in daily life can start with simple yet powerful gestures that affirm the value of those around us. For instance, a sincere compliment to a colleague on a well-done presentation or a thoughtful note to a friend who helped you in a time of need can reinforce your appreciation for their efforts and qualities. Here's how you can weave appreciation into the fabric of everyday life:

1. **Verbal Affirmations:** Make it a habit to verbally acknowledge and appreciate the people in your life. For example, telling a family member, "I really appreciate how you always take the time to listen," shows them that you value and love them.

2. **Thoughtful Gestures:** Small acts of kindness, like bringing your partner their favorite coffee on a busy morning or sending a 'thank you' card to someone who offered you support, are tangible ways to express gratitude and strengthen relationships.

3. **Acknowledging Publicly:** When appropriate, publicly acknowledging someone's efforts, such as praising a team member during a meeting for their hard work, not only boosts their morale but also encourages a culture of appreciation within the group.

Real-Life Example of Appreciation's Impact:

Elena, a school teacher who started a gratitude circle in her classroom, encouraged her students at the end of each week to share something they appreciated about their classmates. This practice not only uplifted the class atmosphere but also helped students recognize and articulate the good in others, fostering a supportive and interconnected community. The ripple effects were profound—students reported feeling happier and more connected to their peers, and instances of conflicts decreased.

SUMMARY

- **Cultivating Gratitude**:

  - **Gratitude Journaling**: Begin a gratitude journal to consistently acknowledge and appreciate small joys, enhancing overall happiness.

  - **Expressing Thanks**: Make it a habit to thank people, enhancing your relationships and spreading positivity.

  - **Integrating Mindfulness and Appreciation**: Implementing daily practices of mindfulness to appreciate the present can significantly increase awareness and contentment.

- **Building a Positive Mindset:**

  - **Cultivating Positive Self-Talk**: Regularly use uplifting statements about yourself and your abilities to shift your internal dialogue in a more positive direction.

  - **Cognitive Reframing**: Learn to reframe challenges as opportunities for growth and learning.

  - **Embracing Optimism in Challenges**: Adopt an optimistic outlook to transform obstacles into growth opportunities, enhancing resilience and emotional strength.

- **Nurturing Your Environment:**

  - **Surrounding Yourself with Positivity**: Immerse yourself in uplifting content, relationships and activities that nourish an optimistic mindset.

  - **Prioritizing Self-Care**: Make time for practices like mindfulness, creative outlets and fulfilling hobbies to recharge and relieve stress.

- **Enhancing Connections through Appreciation:**

  - **Everyday Appreciation**: Integrate simple acts of appreciation into daily interactions to strengthen bonds and enrich relationships.

  - **Public Acknowledgment**: Use public praise to boost morale and foster a culture of appreciation.

CHAPTER SIX

HOLISTIC WELLNESS

NURTURING BODY, MIND, AND SOUL

Starting on the wellness journey is a lot like tending to a garden. Just as a garden needs care in every nook and cranny, our pursuit of well-being calls for a balanced focus on our body, mind, and spirit. This path illuminates the idea that being healthy isn't just about not being sick; it's about nurturing our happiness, bouncing back from difficulties, and finding peace within ourselves. Central to this quest is a holistic perspective, acknowledging that each slice of our existence impacts our overall state of health. Imagining our well-being as a flourishing garden, it takes a mix of physical exercise, mental strength, and a connection with our deeper selves to thrive, akin to how a garden needs just the right amount of sunshine, water, and good soil.

However, keeping this equilibrium is quite a task in our rush-rush world. Our day-to-day responsibilities often bump self-care down the priority list, leaving us caught in a whirlwind of stress, subpar eating habits, not enough rest, and a disconnect from our spiritual side. This rift harms not only our body but dims the shine of our mental and spiritual health too. It can feel daunting, trying to figure out where to start or how to fit wellness into our hectic schedules. The real challenge isn't in the scarcity of options for well-being, but in weaving these practices into our daily lives in ways that are straightforward and doable.

VITALIZING PHYSICAL HEALTH

Starting our journey towards complete well-being is about embracing a full-circle approach to taking care of our body, mind, and soul. Within the wide range of options for maintaining our health, physical wellness is a key component that supports our overall energy and vitality. Let's talk about how incorporating regular physical activities, eating right, ensuring we get enough sleep, and finding time to relax is critical for living our happiest and healthiest lives.

Think of regular exercise as your secret weapon for feeling fantastic. When we work out, our body releases endorphins, those wonderful chemicals that create a sense of joy and well-being after a good session of moving our bodies. But it's not only about the immediate happiness boost; it's about sustaining a vibrant and energetic life. Consistency is your best friend here, along with choosing an activity you genuinely enjoy. Whether you're into fast-paced walks, swimming, riding your bike, grooving to music, or using your VR with, for example, Les Mills Bodycombat, aim to hit the recommended 150 minutes of moderate exercise a week, just like the Centers for Disease Control and Prevention suggests. By weaving exercise into our daily plans, we pave the way for better moods, increased energy, and stronger bodies.

Another great option to stay active is incorporating a treadmill at your workplace. I highly recommend this in combination with a height-adjustable desk. While it might not be possible or suitable for everyone, it's worth checking out as it allows for light exercise throughout your workday, helping to maintain energy levels and concentration.

Now, let's shift focus to what's on our plate because the link between our diet and our feelings is massive. Think of your body as a high-performance vehicle that thrives on premium fuel. This doesn't mean cutting out all the foods you love in the name of health. It's all about feeling energized, improving your mood, and keeping your spirits up. Try to eat a rainbow of fruits and veggies, whole grains, and lean proteins while staying hydrated. These steps are not just good for your body but also for your brain, helping you stay sharp and ready to take on whatever comes your way.

Don't forget the power of a good night's sleep in your wellness toolkit. Quality zzz's give our bodies the downtime needed to repair and get ready for another day. Strive for seven to nine hours of peaceful sleep each night, and consider establishing a relaxing bedtime routine that could include reading or gentle stretches. Make your bedroom a sleep sanctuary by keeping it quiet, dark, and cool. Good sleep habits are a major player in the game of well-being, significantly impacting our physical and emotional health.

Moreover, finding peace in the hustle and bustle of everyday life is crucial. Practices like yoga or meditation are effective ways to reduce stress and boost our physical health by making us more flexible, easing muscle tension, and helping maintain a healthy blood pressure. And you don't have to dedicate hours to see benefits; even short sessions can make a big difference. Begin with easy breathing exercises or simple yoga poses and gradually build them into your daily life.

BUILDING MENTAL RESILIENCE

Delving into the world of mental health feels a bit like walking through a maze. It's not always straightforward and at times can be tricky, but with a dose of patience, some empathy, and a handful of good strategies, navigating it becomes easier. Among these strategies, mindfulness emerges as a shining beacon. It's like finding a calm spot in the middle of a storm where you can breathe deeply and stay centered. This magical ability to remain anchored in the now helps us manage stress and cultivates an optimistic mindset, opening doors to personal growth and happiness.

To weave mindfulness seamlessly into your daily life, here are a few steps to consider:

- For beginners, a helpful technique is to slowly count from 20 to 1 in your mind, then start the count over from 20 again. As mentioned before, this can be coupled with breath, but you can also count very slowly without synchronizing with your exhaling. This method helps maintain focus and enhances the effectiveness of your meditation time.

- Try mindful eating; really savor every bite of your meal, noticing the flavors, textures, and how it makes your body feel. This doesn't just make meals more enjoyable but also helps with feeling full.

- Bring mindfulness into simple daily activities, like taking a shower or going for a walk. Immersing yourself fully in these actions allows you to experience them on a deeper level.

In addition to mindfulness, cognitive behavioral techniques (CBT) offer a structured approach to building mental resilience. CBT involves training ourselves to notice negative thought patterns and actively challenge them. It's like being a detective in your own mind, questioning thoughts that bring you down and replacing them with truthful, positive ones. This technique builds on the concept of positive self-talk introduced in the previous chapter but goes further by providing tools to break free from detrimental perceptions, guiding us toward a brighter, more positive outlook on life.

Here's how you can incorporate CBT into your everyday life:

- Keep an eye on your thoughts, recognize they're there, but don't take them at face value.

- Question those negative or unhelpful thoughts by looking for real evidence against them.

- Gradually swap out irrational thoughts with truthful, positive ones, teaching your brain to default to optimism.

This practice of actively replacing negative thoughts with positive, truthful ones can be tremendously powerful. One practical way to reinforce it is to use daily routines as cues for this cognitive reframing. For example, you can take advantage of bathroom breaks as private moments to consciously repeat your new positive affirmations.

Moreover, each time the old, pessimistic thought tries to invade your peace, replace it immediately with your positive affirmation. Ensure that the tone of this inner voice is kind, understanding, and supportive—qualities that are critical to making the affirmation feel genuine and effective. This practice can transform your overall mood and outlook significantly.

For instance, consider Tom, who frequently doubted his creativity at work. He decided to affirm, "I am full of creativity and my ideas are valuable," each time he recognized his negative self-talk creeping in. Importantly, Tom began this practice during his daily bathroom breaks, using those moments to remind himself of his new narrative. Over time, this not only helped in reinforcing the positive affirmation but also in making such uplifting thoughts a natural part of his internal dialogue.

Sometimes, we might forget to replace a negative thought right when it appears, and that's okay. Establishing the habit of using routines like bathroom breaks as a cue to think positively helps maintain this practice. Each time you sit down, quietly say the positive sentence in your mind. This simple act can greatly enhance your life quality and happiness by gradually altering the nature of your internal conversations.

By dedicating ourselves to the CBT method, we can develop a more positive, supportive inner voice that enhances our resilience and overall well-being.

Understanding when it's time to seek professional help plays a critical role in managing our mental well-being too. Admitting you need support shows incredible strength and courage. Sometimes, the load is too heavy to lift by ourselves, and that's perfectly okay. Professional help can offer customized strategies that go beyond what we can do solo, supporting us in ways we hadn't imagined.

In addition to these strategies, immersing yourself in creative activities or hobbies provides a therapeutic outlet for release and relaxation. Whether it's through painting, writing, gardening, or any form of creativity that speaks to you, these activities act as vents for expressing feelings and melting away stress. They're essential pieces of our mental wellness puzzle, bringing joy and a sense of achievement outside the regular grind.

CULTIVATING SPIRITUAL WELL-BEING

Venturing into the world of spiritual well-being, we uncover a treasure trove of opportunities to boost not only our health but also our joy. This journey goes beyond taking care of our bodies or managing our emotional highs and lows; it's about caring for our spirit, that deep, often unspoken part of us. At first, this may seem a bit out there or overwhelming, yet embarking on this path is deeply personal and incredibly fulfilling. Let's explore how finding our purpose, engaging in spiritual rituals, connecting with nature, and reflecting on what we hold dear can immensely enrich our holistic wellness.

Embarking on a quest to find and nurture our life's purpose isn't something that happens overnight. It's an ongoing adventure that calls for reflection, a dash of curiosity, and bravery. Having a purpose steers us, while finding meaning in what we do gives us the enthusiasm to keep moving forward. Begin by pondering what's truly important to you. Ask yourself about your passions and the mark you wish to leave on the world. These inquiries are stepping stones towards uncovering your unique journey, bolstering your resilience, and enhancing your overall well-being along the way.

Additionally, practices like meditation and prayer offer a profound sense of serenity and connection. These quiet moments of introspection help us pause the daily hustle and touch base with something larger than ourselves. If meditation is new to you, try starting with just a few minutes each day, focusing on your breathing, like it was mentioned before. And then slowly extend the time as you get more comfortable. Prayer, too, can be a potent means of expressing gratitude, seeking guidance, and celebrating one's faith, no matter the religious affiliation.

Moreover, immersing ourselves in nature presents another avenue toward spiritual wellness. The natural world has this incredible power to heal, motivate, and reconnect us to our very essence. Whether through a stroll in a park, tending to a garden, or just sitting quietly under a tree, these acts provide space for meditation and spiritual contemplation. They remind us of the wonder and interconnection of all life, fostering a sense of holistic health that goes beyond the physical.

Reflecting on our personal values and beliefs is key to living in harmony with our deepest selves, nurturing spiritual growth. When our actions mirror our inner convictions, we lead lives filled with integrity and satisfaction. It helps to occasionally evaluate your values and beliefs, maybe by journaling or chatting with close friends or mentors. Such reflective habits help deepen our understanding of ourselves and encourage living authentically according to our principles.

The role of spirituality in healthcare and in our everyday lives is paramount. A study by researchers at Harvard T.H. Chan School of Public Health (The President and Fellows of Harvard College, 2022) emphasizes the need to integrate spirituality in managing serious illnesses and in promoting general health. This extensive review points to a link between spirituality and improved health outcomes, advocating for care that considers the whole person, including their spiritual needs.

Integrating spiritual well-being into our lives brings wide-ranging benefits. Delving into our values and beliefs, embracing spiritual routines, connecting with the environment, and seeking inner congruity doesn't just elevate our spiritual health but also boosts our resilience, peace, and contentment. In a society fixated on external accomplishments, prioritizing our spiritual health provides balance, anchoring us in the essence of what really matters.

INTEGRATING HOLISTIC PRACTICES

Taking care of ourselves in a holistic way is akin to tending to a garden. Imagine how a lush garden thrives with the right mix of water, sunlight, and fertile soil. In a similar vein, our wellbeing flourishes when we nurture our bodies, minds, and spirits. But let's face it, weaving these practices into the fabric of our busy lives can be tough. Yet, it's absolutely essential for our overall health and happiness. Here are some gentle steps to guide you in fostering a well-rounded self-care routine:

Start by pinpointing physical activities you enjoy, like yoga or swimming, and make them a part of your weekly agenda. It's about moving your body in ways that feel good to you. Next, carve out moments for mental recharge – this could be journaling or diving into a hobby that brings you peace. Don't forget the spiritual dimension, whether that means meditation or immersing yourself in nature. This will vary widely, as spirituality is deeply personal. And remember, seeking balance is crucial. Avoid overwhelming yourself with too many changes at once. Begin with small, manageable steps and let your self-care regimen evolve naturally.

> This approach of starting small and gradually incorporating different self-care practices is key throughout this book. With so much information and techniques shared, it can be tempting to try to do everything at once. However, real, lasting change rarely happens that way. Instead, take the time to explore the various possibilities presented, and choose one or two that resonate with you to begin implementing into your life. Don't just read and contemplate - take action. Once those initial practices become integrated habits, you can then explore adding new techniques or adjusting your routine. The goal is to build a sustainable, holistic self-care regimen at a comfortable pace. So read, choose activities mindfully, put them into practice, reassess, and continue adapting.

Setting aside time for self-care doesn't mean micromanaging every second of your day. Instead, it's about ensuring you have sacred moments amid the chaos, specifically reserved for you. Treat these self-care appointments with the same seriousness you would any key meeting. Whether it's carving out time in the early hours, sneaking in moments during lunch, or unwinding in the evening, find what suits you and guard this time zealously. Consistency here is key, as regularity turns actions into habits, and habits form the backbone of wellbeing. This approach is supported by recommendations from the Cleveland Clinic (n.d.).

Mindfulness transforms ordinary experiences into extraordinary moments of awareness and equilibrium. It's about fully enjoying that morning coffee, relishing the sensation of water in a shower, or listening intently to a friend without thinking about your response. Rather than being another item on your checklist, mindfulness allows you to live life more richly, connecting deeply with the present moment. This practice not only sharpens mental focus but also helps alleviate stress, leading to a more harmonious life.

Creating a supportive community is much like crafting a safety net that's there to catch you when you stumble and elevate you during your high points. Encircle yourself with folks who value holistic wellness - those who actively pursue their own health and inspire you to do the same. This network might emerge in traditional locales like fitness centers and yoga studios, or within digital forums focused on health and wellness. The key is in the shared encouragement, experiences, and accountability that keep you inspired and grounded.

Embarking on a holistic self-care journey, committing daily time for self-care, engaging in mindfulness, and cultivating a supportive network are essential aspects of well-being. They represent meaningful investments in your most precious asset - yourself. As the Cleveland Clinic notes, integrative medicine underscores the importance of the patient-provider partnership in healing (Cleveland Clinic, n.d.). This perspective mirrors how we should approach self-care, treating ourselves with compassion and cooperation akin to what we would expect from a healthcare provider. Recognizing that our wellness is multi-dimensional is crucial; paying equal attention to our physical, mental, and spiritual needs.

Navigating the pursuit of a balanced lifestyle, especially in an era marked by constant upheaval, is undoubtedly daunting. Yet, it's a profoundly rewarding endeavor. By heeding these suggestions, we not only enhance our own wellbeing but also contribute to a larger movement towards health and happiness. This method resonates with my conviction that balancing personal efforts with community support is essential, grounded in practices proven to prioritize human well-being above all else.

As we strive for balance, we see how our own health is linked to our community's health. This connection underscores the importance of a healthcare system that reflects the diversity and complexity of its users. While everyone's approach to holistic practices may vary, one thing remains constant: taking care of all aspects of our health is essential, not just a luxury.

TRANSFORMING LIFE THROUGH HOLISTIC WELLNESS

Embarking on a journey toward total well-being is a bit like tending to a garden. Imagine nurturing every aspect of yourself with the same attention and care you would give to growing plants. You need sunlight, water, and good soil for a garden to thrive. Similarly, our overall health flourishes when we feed it with regular physical exercise, mental fortitude, spiritual connection, and self-love every single day. This path of holistic wellness is an adventure filled with self-discovery and empowerment, prompting us to look after every piece of who we are.

It's crucial to understand that adopting a holistic approach to life isn't solely for our own benefit. Its impact goes far beyond, touching the hearts and lives of those we interact with, helping build a world brimming with joy and wellness. The journey towards maintaining balance in our lives sends out waves that reach our communities and weave into the societal fabric, bringing positive change and harmony.

SUMMARY

- **Vitalize Physical Health**:

  - **Exercise Regularly**: Incorporate 150 minutes of moderate exercise per week to enhance mood and energy.

  - **Eat Nutritiously**: Focus on a balanced diet rich in fruits, vegetables, whole grains, and lean proteins.

  - **Prioritize Sleep**: Aim for 7-9 hours of quality sleep per night and establish a calming bedtime routine.

  - **Relax and Unwind**: Engage in stress-reducing activities such as yoga or meditation to maintain physical and mental health.

- **Build Mental Resilience**:

  - **Practice Mindfulness**: Integrate mindfulness into daily activities like eating and walking to enhance focus and reduce stress.

  - **Use Cognitive Behavioral Techniques (CBT)**: Monitor and adjust your thoughts to foster a positive mindset.

  - **Seek Professional Help When Needed**: Recognize the strength in seeking support to manage mental health challenges.

- ○ **Engage in Creative Activities**: Incorporate hobbies that provide emotional release and relaxation.

- **Cultivate Spiritual Well-being**:

  - ○ **Explore Spirituality**: Whether through meditation, prayer, or nature, connect with your inner self and the larger universe.

  - ○ **Reflect on Personal Values**: Regularly assess and align your actions with your deepest beliefs and ethics.

  - ○ **Find and Nurture Purpose**: Determine what drives you and pursue activities that align with your passions and goals.

- **Integrate Holistic Practices into Daily Life**:

  - ○ **Set Realistic Goals**: Start with small, achievable steps to incorporate physical, mental, and spiritual practices into your routine.

  - ○ **Create a Supportive Environment**: Surround yourself with a community that values and practices holistic wellness.

  - ○ **Prioritize Consistent Self-Care**: Treat self-care with the same importance as other critical appointments in your life.

CHAPTER SEVEN

STRENGTHENING RESILIENCE IN ADVERSITY

When life throws challenges our way, finding our inner strength can lead to profound transformation. It's like steering through a storm; developing resilience gives us the tools and knowledge to not only make it out alive but to come out stronger. This process involves tapping into a hidden strength, cultivating an unstoppable spirit that won't be crushed by setbacks and carves a new path of growth and toughness.

Life's tough moments can often make us feel adrift in a vast ocean, trying desperately to stay afloat. Whether we're dealing with the pain of personal loss, career hiccups, or emotional distress, these trials push our limits and threaten to wash away our hope and self-esteem. At times like these, the idea of being resilient might seem too far out of reach, almost like a mirage. Without someone to show us the way or lend a helping hand, trying to pick up the pieces and rebuild after such trials can seem overwhelming, filling us with uncertainty about our ability to bounce back and move ahead. This strain underlines a significant need in our journey for personal betterment—a call for practical advice and insights that enable us to sail through these stormy periods with poise and resolve.

UNDERSTANDING THE CONCEPT OF RESILIENCE

Grasping the essence of resilience is a bit like appreciating the quiet power that helps us weather not just real storms, but also the figurative ones life throws our way. It's that deep-seated strength that allows people to recover from setbacks and adapt with a positive outlook when things change, giving them a feeling of control when life gets chaotic. Resilience isn't a magical trait available only to a select few; it's more like a muscle—something you can build and strengthen over time through dedication and hard work.

Resilience means viewing challenges not as barriers, but as opportunities to grow and learn. By changing your perspective this way, you build a mindset that keeps you pushing forward, even during hard times. To build resilience, it's important to see challenges as opportunities to strengthen ourselves. This idea is supported by the Center on the Developing Child at Harvard University (2020), which notes that facing challenges directly is essential for growth. Understanding that we can develop resilience gives us a powerful sense of freedom and optimism, helping us navigate tough times and emerge stronger and more capable.

But remember, building up your resilience doesn't mean going it alone or keeping your struggles to yourself. Here's how you can actively cultivate resilience:

- Start by spending time on relationships that uplift and support you. Having people in your corner offers a layer of protection against the stresses of life, giving you emotional and practical backup whenever you need it.

- Next, boost your confidence in your own abilities. Trusting in your power to affect your life positively is fundamental.

- Then, look for and take part in situations that push you to adapt and manage yourself better. This not only builds resilience but enriches your character.

- Lastly, never underestimate how beneficial positive experiences and coping methods can be when faced with tough times.

Understanding what fuels resilience, like meaningful connections and self-confidence, significantly improves how well you handle life's ups and downs. By intentionally focusing on actions and thoughts that nurture these qualities, you can greatly beef up your resilience score.

Part of becoming more resilient involves reinterpreting setbacks as opportunities for personal progress. It takes patience and continuous effort to adopt this mindset, but the payoff is immense, offering a deeply empowering way to face life's hurdles. This transformative stance makes each challenge an opportunity for growth rather than a roadblock to happiness.

Adopting such a resilient outlook helps us flourish during tough times. Viewing difficulties as essential for personal growth allows us to discover strengths we didn't know we possessed. This journey might not always be smooth or pain-free, but it's often through overcoming these hardships that we uncover our true capabilities and resilience.

Interestingly, research from the Center on the Developing Child at Harvard University (2020) reinforces that resilience is dynamic and can be developed throughout one's life, not merely in youth or childhood. This insight is encouraging, reminding us that it's never too late to work on our resilience. Whether it's through physical activity, reducing stress, or participating in programs aimed at improving self-regulation, there are plenty of valid, science-backed strategies to enhance our resilience at any age.

Personal Example:
Emily's Journey Through Adversity

Meet Emily, a community nurse whose resilience was put to the test when her town was hit by a severe flood. Overnight, her life and the lives of her neighbors were turned upside down. With her community in chaos and her own home at risk, Emily faced a stark choice: succumb to despair or harness her inner strength.

Choosing the latter, Emily found new depths of resilience. Each day, she focused on what she could control—organizing relief efforts, providing medical care, and supporting her neighbors. Her perspective on challenges as opportunities for growth transformed her approach to the crisis. She saw each obstacle as a chance to learn and strengthen her capabilities, not just for herself but for her community.

As Emily navigated the recovery efforts, she relied heavily on her network of friends, family, and colleagues. This support system was crucial, providing both emotional backing and practical help.

Emily also took time to reflect on her achievements each day, no matter how small, which bolstered her confidence and reaffirmed her effectiveness in managing tough situations.

Months later, as the community began to rebuild, Emily emerged not only as a key figure in the recovery but also as a stronger and more capable leader. Her story exemplifies how embracing resilience—seeing challenges as opportunities, leaning on others for support, and believing in one's own abilities—can lead to profound personal and community growth.

DEVELOPING COPING STRATEGIES FOR TOUGH TIMES

Life's journey is both beautiful and filled with uncertainties. We all face moments that truly test our endurance and inner strength. During these times, it becomes essential to have coping strategies in place. Recognizing the importance of healthy ways to deal with life's struggles is the first step. Activities like physical exercise or mindfulness aren't just trendy topics. They are proven by research to have a profound effect on our mental health, giving us a much-needed boost. Exercise sends a rush of endorphins through our body, lifting our spirits, while mindfulness anchors us in the here and now, easing stress and worry.

Having a circle of support is fundamental during tough periods. The presence of friends, family, or professionals ready to offer a shoulder to lean on is priceless. Their support and guidance can be the light at the end of a dark tunnel. Here's how you can strengthen your support network:

- Make it a point to keep in touch with those you care about.

- Look into joining groups where you'll find others who understand what you're going through.

- Seeking professional advice is a strong move, never a weakness.

Self-care is your shield against challenges, with sleep, good nutrition, and relaxation being the pillars that uphold your well-being. Making sure you get enough rest, eat well, and find ways to unwind is crucial for both your physical and mental health. Creating routines around these practices, like setting a regular bedtime, enjoying wholesome meals, and discovering relaxation methods that bring you joy, lays the groundwork for resilience.

It's also critical to know when to seek help—it shows courage and self-awareness. Realizing that we all need a helping hand at times is key to building a stronger self.

Adapting these strategies into our daily lives isn't an overnight task. It involves making small, steady changes that add up significantly over time. Research from Mental Health America highlights that those who write about their struggles or adopt proactive problem-solving techniques tend to experience better health outcomes and lower depression rates. This tells us that actively engaging in coping mechanisms can genuinely enhance our mental wellness.

Building resilience is a gradual process, a journey of equipping ourselves with the right tools to face life's hurdles confidently. The current global scenario, rife with division and uncertainty, further highlights the urgency for resilience. By opting for strategies grounded in evidence, we can tread through these challenging times with dignity and poise.

The approaches we've talked about go beyond mere suggestions—they are strategies supported by scientific research and real-world effectiveness. Embracing them doesn't erase obstacles but prepares us to navigate through them more adeptly. It's all about gearing up for life's inevitable roller-coaster rides, ensuring we emerge stronger after every twist and turn.

Recognizing our individual paths through adversity is crucial. What helps one person may not suit another, and that's completely fine. The idea is to approach these strategies with an open mind and tailor them to our unique situations. Finding what clicks for you and taking steps, no matter how small, towards becoming a resilient person is what matters most.

By adopting these coping methods, we're not only helping ourselves but also lighting the way for others. Sharing our stories and the tactics that helped us can encourage those around us to find their path through tough times. It's about creating a chain reaction of resilience and well-being that reaches far beyond our immediate circle.

Let's view these strategies as more than tips; let's see them as commitments to our well-being and to each other. In doing so, we're not just navigating through the storm; we're learning to thrive amidst it. With dedication, patience, and a deep-seated empathy for our shared human experiences, we can overcome any obstacle and come to appreciate life's intricate tapestry even more.

LEARNING FROM FAILURES
AND BOUNCING BACK

Learning to see failure as not just an unavoidable part of life but as incredibly valuable lessons can truly change how powerful and free we feel. This idea that failing isn't the opposite of success, but actually a step towards it, encourages us to look at our setbacks in a whole new light. Here's a little guide on how to shift your perception and deal with failure more effectively:

First off, it's okay to acknowledge how you're feeling when you fail. It's natural to be disappointed, upset, or frustrated. What's important is not to dwell too much on these feelings. After giving yourself some time to process, take a step back and try to objectively figure out what didn't work out and why. This is a key step in turning a tough situation into a lesson for the future. Then, think about what you've learned and come up with concrete steps to make things better moving forward.

Remember, failures don't define who you are; it's how you respond to them that really shows your character. Looking back on past challenges with a mix of critical thinking and compassion helps us learn important lessons (Colorado State University. , n. d.). This way of thinking not only gets us ready for future hurdles but also makes us more adaptable, which is crucial given how fast everything around us is constantly changing.

Being kind to ourselves during tough times plays a huge role in how quickly and effectively we can bounce back from failure. Showing yourself the same kindness and understanding you'd show a good friend can make a big difference in your emotional well-being. Here are a couple of tips on practicing self-compassion:

Talk to yourself like you would to a friend who's going through a rough patch, with encouragement and empathy. Understand that everyone fails sometimes, and it's a part of being human. You're definitely not alone in feeling down. Also, don't forget to do things that make you feel good physically, emotionally, and mentally.

Embracing kindness towards ourselves not only eases the pain of defeat but also equips us to handle future difficulties with a healthier and stronger mindset (Neff, Hsieh, & Dejitterat, 2005).

Another helpful way to look at failure is to see it as a temporary roadblock rather than a final stop. This attitude encourages us to keep going and maintains our hope during tough times. Here's what you can do:

Remind yourself of past obstacles you've overcome. This helps strengthen your belief in your own resilience. If needed, tweak your goals, but don't give up on them entirely. Sometimes, failure just means you need a new strategy, not that you should stop trying. And don't forget to celebrate your small wins along the way. They help maintain enthusiasm and morale, even when things aren't going according to plan.

This outlook fosters perseverance and resilience, reminding us that setbacks are not forever—they're just steps on the path to greater achievements.

To turn failures into opportunities for growth, it helps to reflect, practice self-kindness, and keep looking forward. By seeing failures as valuable lessons, forgiving ourselves, and viewing setbacks as temporary hiccups, we develop a stronger and more adaptable mindset. Such an approach doesn't remove the sting of defeat or promise instant victories, but it builds a solid base for a more rewarding journey through life's highs and lows.

Personal Example: Angela's Startup Setback

Meet Angela, a budding entrepreneur who launched a mobile app startup with high hopes. Within the first year, despite her enthusiasm and hard work, Angela faced a significant setback: her app did not gain the traction she had anticipated, and funding was dwindling fast. The failure hit hard, and Angela found herself grappling with feelings of self-doubt and frustration.

However, Angela chose to see this failure not as a defeat but as a vital learning opportunity. She took some time to process her emotions and then conducted a thorough analysis of what went wrong. Angela realized that her marketing strategy was not aligned with her target audience's preferences, which was a crucial oversight.

Determined to turn her setback into a stepping stone, Angela reached out to a mentor for advice and adjusted her approach. She revamped her marketing strategy to better resonate with her audience and slowly began to see improved engagement. During this time, Angela made it a point to practice self-compassion, reminding herself that every entrepreneur faces challenges and that persistence and resilience are key.

Over time, Angela's startup began to recover. She not only learned valuable lessons about business strategy but also about the importance of resilience and adaptability. Angela's story is a testament to the power of viewing failures as opportunities for growth, maintaining self-compassion, and persistently working towards one's goals.

FOSTERING A GROWTH
MINDSET FOR RESILIENCE

Believing that we all have the untapped potential to better ourselves and enhance our skills is the key to nurturing a mindset geared towards growth. At its core, this belief revolves around the idea that our abilities and intelligence are not static but can grow with time through hard work, dedication, and persistence. This empowering viewpoint inspires us to view setbacks not as roadblocks but as opportunities for reaching new heights.

The journey starts by welcoming challenges with open arms. Instead of seeing them as threats or signs of defeat, we should recognize them as chances to learn and develop ourselves further. This change in perspective alters how we emotionally react to tough situations, fostering resilience as a more instinctive response to life's inevitable ups and downs. By accepting challenges, we shake off the fear of failure, a crucial move for anyone looking to build a resilient and progressive way of thinking.

Moreover, it's important to pay attention to the conversations we have with ourselves during times of stress or disappointment. Engaging in positive self-talk can dramatically change how we see our own abilities. Transforming thoughts from "I'm just not good enough" to "I didn't make it this time, but I gained valuable lessons for the future" encourages a kinder and more constructive stance towards self-improvement and resilience. Adopting a language that supports growth, such as "mistakes help me learn," fosters a mentality ready to embrace learning and development, no matter the obstacles (Parrish, 2022).

Setting achievable goals and breaking them into smaller, manageable tasks is crucial for building resilience. Celebrating these small wins boosts our sense of progress and achievement, propelling our motivation and deepening our commitment to our main goals. Here's how you can apply this thinking:

- Begin with defining clear, reachable goals related to your long-term dreams.

- Divide these goals into finite, doable actions that you can execute regularly.

- Acknowledge the completion of these actions, viewing each as a stride closer to your ultimate aim.

This structured method doesn't just promote a growth mindset by underscoring personal development's step-by-step nature; it also clarifies the route towards fulfilling complex objectives, making them appear more accessible.

Nurturing a growth mindset isn't something you do alone; it thrives in an environment filled with support. Parents, teachers, and mentors play a vital role in encouraging this mindset by exemplifying resilient behaviors, offering useful feedback, and valuing effort as well as results. Promoting risk-taking, focusing on learning rather than merely dodging failure, and stressing the importance of endurance are all essential in creating a culture that champions growth and resilience.

Additionally, introducing the concept of neuroplasticity — the brain's amazing capacity to forge new connections and pathways when we learn and experience new things — to both kids and adults enhances the understanding that our brains and, subsequently, our abilities are malleable. This knowledge fortifies the conviction that our talents are not carved in stone but can expand with effort and determination.

SUMMARY

- **Understand Resilience as a Skill**:

  - Recognize resilience as a muscle that can be developed with practice.

  - View challenges as opportunities to grow, enhancing your ability to bounce back stronger.

- **Cultivate Supportive Relationships**:

  - Build and maintain close connections that provide emotional and practical support.

  - Trust in your abilities and engage in activities that challenge and grow your skills.

- **Adopt a Positive Outlook**:

  - Shift your perspective to see difficulties as learning opportunities.

  - Use positive experiences and effective coping methods to handle stress and adversity.

- **Engage in Physical and Mindfulness Practices**:

  - Incorporate regular exercise and mindfulness to manage stress and improve mental health.

- Recognize the importance of a supportive circle and professional help when needed.

- **Develop Coping Strategies**:

  - Establish healthy routines for sleep, nutrition, and relaxation.

  - Use resilience-building practices like physical activity and stress reduction techniques regularly.

- **Learn from Failures**:

  - Embrace failures as lessons and opportunities for growth.

  - Practice self-compassion and adjust your goals and strategies as needed.

- **Foster a Growth Mindset**:

  - Embrace challenges and view them as chances to learn and develop.

  - Engage in positive self-talk and set achievable goals to foster persistence and resilience.

- **Implement Practical Resilience Strategies**:

  - Break down large goals into manageable tasks and celebrate small achievements.

  - Surround yourself with a supportive community that encourages growth and resilience.

CHAPTER EIGHT

SELF-COMPASSION

EMBRACING KINDNESS AND ACCEPTANCE

Growing an attitude of self-compassion is akin to tending a garden within our souls, where we nurture the seeds of kindness and acceptance until they flourish in every aspect of our lives. This vital practice builds a supportive relationship with ourselves, one that acts as the cornerstone for enduring mental health. In those quiet moments just before dawn breaks, affirming our own value can brighten our entire day, much like the first light of the sun. By consistently recognizing our accomplishments and efforts, we embed a deep sense of self-respect and love in our hearts, creating an internal ally rather than an enemy. This kind inner voice becomes our steadfast friend through all of life's fluctuations, pushing us to approach each day with bravery and poise.

Yet, there are numerous challenges in keeping up this compassionate inner conversation. We often lean towards criticizing ourselves for even the smallest mistakes or hiccups, which casts a long shadow over our journey toward self-kindness. It's all too easy to fall into a spiral of negative self-talk, focusing on our shortcomings rather than our achievements, which diminishes our ability to feel joy and satisfaction. This relentless chase for perfection saps our energy, leaving us with little capacity to appreciate the beauty in our own imperfections. The real issue, therefore, isn't our stumble but the tough way we respond to these slip-ups, which can wear down our mental well-being and block our path to a rewarding life.

In this section, we aim to shed light on how embodying kindness and acceptance can fundamentally change how we view ourselves. We'll delve into actionable steps for ending the cycle of self-criticism by building resilience against the inevitable snags we find in our way, and by fostering a mindset that sees errors not as failures but as chances to grow. By treating ourselves with the same tenderness we would show to a cherished friend, we unlock the potential for a more tender existence. Engaging in mindful practices, taking time for self-care, and pardoning our own past mistakes sets the stage for developing a deeper, more empathetic bond with ourselves and, consequently, with others around us.

PRACTICING SELF-KINDNESS AND UNDERSTANDING

In our fast-moving lives, it's easy to forget the importance of being kind and understanding toward ourselves. Starting our days by recognizing what we're good at and our small victories can make a huge difference in how we feel mentally. This act of self-recognition serves as a morning boost, helping us see ourselves and our abilities in a more positive light. Here's a straightforward way to make this part of your daily routine:

- When you wake up, take a deep breath and find your calm.

- Think about what you've achieved recently, no matter how minor, and either say it out loud or write it down.

- Remind yourself of your strengths and the special traits that make you, well, you.

- Decide to maintain this positive view of yourself all day.

Now, picture how you'd comfort a friend who's having a tough time. You'd probably be supportive and kind, right? Try directing that same compassion and kindness toward yourself, especially when things get rough. This practice creates a supportive inner environment that is key for bouncing back emotionally. By treating ourselves as we would a cherished friend, we build up a sense of internal support that boosts our confidence and self-worth.

Also, it's essential to look at our mistakes without being too hard on ourselves. Understanding that making errors is part of being human allows us to learn from them instead of feeling like we've failed. Welcoming our flaws with open arms leads to growth and fosters a forgiving and healthy relationship with ourselves.

Taking care of our needs is another crucial step in creating a loving relationship with ourselves. Whether it's through meditation, exercise, diving into hobbies, or just resting, these acts of self-care nourish our whole being and improve our overall health. The aim is to regularly participate in these self-care activities intentionally.

Self-compassion genuinely benefits our mental health. It's associated with reduced anxiety, depression, and stress, and helps us see ourselves in a more positive and realistic light. Knowing we're not alone in our challenges makes us feel more connected to others and less isolated. Self-compassion has several mental health benefits. While many of us struggle to be kind to ourselves, we can learn to treat ourselves in gentler and more forgiving ways (Harvard Health, 2013; McLean Hospital, n.d.; Self-Compassion.org, 2024).

At its core, practicing self-compassion means offering ourselves the type of care and understanding we would give to someone we love. It involves seeing our value and supporting ourselves through life's inevitable challenges. This approach doesn't mean ignoring our faults or not taking responsibility for our actions. Rather, it encourages us to be gentle and forgiving with ourselves, acknowledging that we cannot be perfect and that mistakes are chances for improvement.

Learning to be compassionate towards ourselves might not come easily, especially if we're used to criticizing ourselves. But, like any skill, it improves with practice and patience. Start by catching yourself when you slip into self-criticism and consciously choose a kinder response. Over time, this kinder way of talking to yourself will likely become more natural, gradually taking over the negative self-talk.

Mindfulness also plays a crucial role in developing self-compassion. By observing our thoughts and feelings without judgment, we allow ourselves to respond with kindness rather than self-criticism. Mindfulness helps us remain present with our experiences, leading us to treat both ourselves and our lives with more acceptance and compassion.

Remember, reaching out for help from friends, family, or professionals is also an act of self-kindness. At times, we all need a bit of assistance to get through tough periods or to learn healthier self-relations. Asking for help shows strength, not weakness, and is a step toward laying down a stronger, more caring foundation for our mental health.

OVERCOMING SELF-CRITICISM THROUGH MINDFULNESS AND COMPASSION

Stepping into the world of self-love and beating down the inner critic is like setting off on a path to a more compassionate, self-understanding you. It goes beyond just silencing that nagging voice inside—it's about changing it from being your biggest doubter into your number one supporter. This change kicks off when we start to question the negativity we often tell ourselves, like "I'm not good enough" or "I'm going to fail," and challenge how true these statements really are.

When those harmful whispers begin to creep in, it's crucial to stop and really think about where they're coming from. Ask yourself, "Is this actually true, or is it just my perception?" More times than not, you'll discover these thoughts aren't based on fact but are rather twisted versions of reality. By switching out negative thoughts with positive affirmations, such as replacing "I always mess up" with "I can learn and grow from my mistakes," you'll see a significant shift in your overall mood and mindset.

Adding self-compassion meditation to your daily routine introduces a fresh way to cultivate a positive mental space. This practice is all about bringing forward feelings of kindness and care towards yourself, much like you would do for a loved one. Here's a simple way to get started:

- Choose a quiet spot where you can be undisturbed.

- Focus on your breathing, paying attention to each breath in and out.

- Picture someone you have strong feelings for and imagine sending them compassion and kindness.

- Gradually turn that compassionate focus inward, showering yourself with that same kindness.

- Reaffirm these feelings by telling yourself wishes of happiness, personal growth, and freedom from pain.

An essential step is to replace self-criticism with words of encouragement and helpful feedback, particularly during tough times. Instead of being hard on yourself for a mistake, recognize your efforts and look at what you can take away from the situation. Encouraging yourself with phrases like, "I did my best, and I'll learn from this," places the emphasis on improvement and moving forward rather than on the mistake itself.

Mindfulness techniques are incredibly effective in managing negative thoughts and feelings. By becoming mindful, you learn to notice your thoughts and emotions without attaching any judgment to them, understanding that they are momentary and do not define your worth. Throughout your day, you can practice mindfulness by:

- Paying close attention to your senses – the feel of water during showers or savoring the taste of your food.

- Watching your thoughts and emotions as they pop up, simply noting them without getting caught up.

- Bringing your mind back to the present whenever it starts to drift.

Adopting these practices helps you develop resilience against self-criticism by nurturing self-compassion and awareness. It shifts your mindset from one of perpetual self-judgment to one filled with understanding and backing. This not only does wonders for your mental health but also equips you to handle the bumps and challenges of life with more calm and confidence.

It's important to remember that building self-compassion is a journey that requires time, patience, and sometimes facing resistance or slipping back into old habits of self-doubt. Nonetheless, making an effort to view yourself through a compassionate lens, similar to how you'd view others, is a profound and life-changing endeavor.

By weaving these strategies into your everyday life, you lay down a foundation of self-kindness that uplifts your mental well-being. It's not solely about dialing down the negative chatter; it's about fostering a peaceful internal environment where self-kindness rules supreme. In today's divided world, taking steps to improve personal well-being carries weight beyond oneself. It involves shaping our inner stories to lead joyous, fulfilled lives and, in turn, positively affecting our surroundings.

EMBRACING IMPERFECTION AND GROWTH THROUGH SELF-ACCEPTANCE

Learning to forgive ourselves for mistakes we've made in the past isn't easy, but it's a crucial step toward achieving a healthier mindset. So often, we are our own worst critics, constantly replaying our errors as though they are all that define us. Yet, if we start to see these mistakes as chances to learn and grow, our view on failure begins to shift. Here's how you can begin this important journey: start by looking back on your mistakes, treating them as necessary steps on your path of personal growth. Then, honestly recognize and sit with any feelings of regret or disappointment to better understand where they're coming from. Remind yourself regularly that it's through our missteps, not perfection, that we grow. Lastly, commit to putting what you've learned into practice, which turns regret into positive, actionable change.

To move away from constant self-criticism, it's vital to let go of the unrealistic aim for perfection. Setting achievable goals plays a big part in this. This means making sure your goals match your abilities and resources. Celebrate each little victory, understanding that it's the journey forward that counts, not achieving some idea of perfection. Embracing this principle not only nurtures self-kindness but also leads to a healthier way of viewing both successes and setbacks.

Embracing our imperfections is a key part of learning to accept ourselves. We all have flaws — they're what make us unique and can be linked to some of our greatest strengths. To get comfortable with this truth, try to focus on what you do well and the achievements you've earned, no matter how small. Remember, chasing perfection is unnecessary. Our quirks and faults are what make us human and deepen our connections with others. Accepting ourselves as we are brings inner peace and a sense of satisfaction.

Moreover, using self-compassion to deal with feelings of guilt or shame is essential for our emotional health. Self-compassion means treating ourselves with the same kindness and understanding we would show a good friend. When faced with guilt or shame, take a moment to offer yourself kindness, whether through comforting words or actions. Acknowledge that you're not alone in feeling this way. Think about how these emotions can guide better decisions in the future instead of letting them impact your self-esteem. Adopting a mindset of compassion allows for self-forgiveness, opening the door to personal growth and emotional strength.

Research backs this up, showing that those who practice self-compassion are more resilient, have a higher sense of self-worth, and are more likely to reach their long-term goals (LCSW, 2023).

Choosing self-compassion doesn't mean settling for less. Instead, it's a sign of strength, allowing us to face our vulnerabilities head-on, with dignity and grace. It pushes us to accept our imperfections without falling into self-pity, promoting a mindset focused on growth, learning, and truly taking care of oneself. This mindset lays a solid foundation for enduring mental health and well-being.

Viewing this from the perspective of someone who appreciates evidence-based solutions and personal freedom, it becomes evident that adopting self-compassion over striving for perfection offers a healthier, more sustainable path to mental wellness. People tend to thrive when they fully embrace themselves, draw lessons from their experiences, and offer mutual support through life's challenges. The divisions observed in today's society often mirror the internal conflicts many face between self-criticism and self-acceptance. Similarly, just as there is advocacy for policies that balance individual rights with the greater good, achieving well-being is best supported by blending personal responsibility with community support.

CELEBRATING ONE'S WORTH AND UNIQUENESS WITH SELF-COMPASSION

Taking a moment to focus on what makes us special - our strengths, abilities, and values - is like stepping into sunlight after days spent in the shadow. The world around us often pushes us toward blending in, making it incredibly easy to forget the unique light we bring to the table. To kickstart your journey of self-reflection, why not dedicate a few minutes each day to celebrate yourself? Scribble down everything you love about you - maybe it's how you've bounced back from tough times, your knack for thinking outside the box, or the warmth and care you extend to friends and strangers alike. Also, pondering over the values steering your life can shed light on your actions and choices, helping sketch a fuller, vibrant picture of who you truly are.

**Practical Exercise:
Celebrating Your Unique Qualities** 

Daily Reflection Journal:

- **Time**: For 5 days, set aside 5-10 minutes each day.

- **What You'll Need**: A notebook or journal and a pen.

Step 1: Strengths and Abilities:

- Write down three things you love about yourself. These can be qualities, skills, or moments you are proud of.

- For example: "I am resilient, I have a creative approach to problem-solving, and I am compassionate."

Step 2: Values Exploration:

- Reflect on and list the values that guide your actions and decisions. Consider how these values influence your life.

- For example: "Integrity, kindness, innovation."

Step 3: Gratitude and Celebration:

- Note down one instance each day where you have lived in alignment with your strengths or values. Celebrate this moment.

- For example: "Today, I showed kindness by helping a colleague with their workload."

Step 4: Visualization:

- Close your eyes and visualize yourself embracing these strengths and values in a moment of success or happiness. Imagine the feelings of pride and joy that accompany this visualization.

Step 5: Affirmations:

- Write down an affirmation or positive statement that reinforces your unique qualities and values.

- For example: "I am resilient, creative, and kind. I bring my unique light to every situation."

By dedicating a few minutes each day to this exercise, you will nurture a deeper appreciation for your unique qualities, build self-confidence, and stay connected to the values that guide your life.

Next up, let's talk about treating ourselves with tenderness through self-compassionate practices. Imagine offering a friend a comforting hug; that's the kind of warmth and kindness you deserve from yourself. How can you wrap yourself in this comfort daily? Start by staying present - relish each moment without harsh self-judgment. Pen down a letter filled with compassion directed at yourself, especially on days when forgiving yourself feels like a tall order. And, swap the voice of criticism in your head with one of encouragement and warmth as if you're cheering on a friend.

It's normal for shadows of doubt to sometimes cloud our sense of worth. When these moments hit, anchoring ourselves in self-appreciation can be our beacon of light. A simple yet profound tool in this battle is keeping a 'success journal.' Every day, jot down even the tiniest wins - be it whipping up a meal, lending an ear to a friend, or ticking off a task at work. This practice validates your strengths and achievements, quieting the whispers of self-doubt.

At the heart of nurturing a positive sense of self are self-love and acceptance. These aren't just buzzwords but vital pillars supporting our mental and emotional sanctuary. Embracing self-love is about welcoming every part of ourselves with open arms – celebrating both our powers and vulnerabilities. Crafting this sanctuary involves setting healthy boundaries, indulging in activities that light up our world, and surrounding ourselves with people who uplift and understand us.

Embarking on this voyage of acknowledging our worth and unique essence through self-compassion and self-affirmation is indeed an adventure filled with ups and downs. Yet, the rewards include a robust, confident, and joy-filled existence. Each small step towards embracing our individuality, practicing kindness towards ourselves, dispelling doubts, and welcoming self-love lays down the stones on the path to enduring well-being.

In today's world, where criticism seems more common than commendation, choosing to nurture kindness within us rebels against the norm, standing tall as a testament to our right to gentle understanding and respect. This quest for self-compassion isn't about sidelining personal growth; rather, it offers a fertile ground for genuine development, anchored in a deep-rooted acceptance and love for oneself while also being open to evolving.

As we tread this path, remember, the magic lies in the little, consistent acts of kindness towards ourselves. Initially, this might feel counterintuitive, maybe even selfish, as we're often taught to put others before ourselves. But research tells us a different story - those who embrace self-kindness report less anxiety and depression, proving its critical role not only in personal fulfillment but in fostering a compassionate society at large.

By weaving these practices into our daily lives, we elevate not just our own happiness but set a living example for others to follow. This pursuit of self-compassion thus transcends personal gain - it becomes a catalyst for wider societal transformation, marrying the idea of personal accountability with collective empathy.

Personal Example: Lisa's Journey to Self-Compassion

Consider Lisa, a graphic designer who struggled with perfectionism and self-doubt. Her career was on an upward trajectory, yet she constantly felt like she wasn't good enough. After a particularly challenging project where nothing seemed to go right, Lisa felt overwhelmed and considered quitting her job.

However, during this low point, Lisa attended a workshop on self-compassion that shifted her perspective dramatically. She learned to recognize her unique talents and began to appreciate the creativity and dedication she brought to her work. Each morning, Lisa started her day by writing down three things she valued about herself and reflected on her positive impact on her team and clients.

Lisa also embraced the practice of treating herself with the same kindness she would offer a friend. When projects didn't go as planned, instead of spiraling into self-criticism, she would write a compassionate letter to herself, acknowledging her efforts and encouraging perseverance. She swapped her internal critic for a cheerleader, reminding herself of past successes and learned lessons.

These changes didn't transform Lisa overnight, but over time, she built a stronger sense of self-worth and resilience. She became more creative and willing to take risks, knowing that each setback was a step towards greater personal and professional growth. Lisa's story illustrates the profound impact that embracing self-compassion can have on a person's life, transforming self-doubt into a celebration of one's own uniqueness and abilities.

As we've explored the concept of self-compassion together, starting from the fundamental belief that being kind to oneself is crucial for our mental and emotional health, this chapter has highlighted how acknowledging our flaws and offering ourselves the same support we'd give a good friend can spark personal growth and enhance our connections with others.

In our modern, hectic lives, where self-judgment often overshadows self-kindness, it's more important than ever to embrace this journey of self-compassion. It's not about being self-centered; rather, it's a way of caring for ourselves so that we can be more present and giving to the people around us. The widespread adoption of such practices could lead to a world that's more empathetic and understanding.

Looking ahead, it's crucial for each of us to think about how cultivating a habit of being compassionate towards ourselves might not just change our own lives for the better but also positively affect those we come into contact with every day. By taking small steps toward treating ourselves with more kindness, we're contributing to a kinder, more compassionate society.

SUMMARY

- **Cultivate a Kind Inner Voice:**

  - Begin each day by acknowledging your achievements and positive traits.

  - Practice talking to yourself with the same kindness and compassion you would offer a good friend.

- **Break the Cycle of Self-Criticism:**

  - Recognize and challenge negative self-talk by questioning its accuracy and replacing it with positive affirmations.

  - Use mindfulness to observe thoughts without judgment, fostering a non-critical awareness of your self-dialogue.

- **Incorporate Mindfulness and Self-Care:**

  - Engage in regular mindfulness practices such as meditation or mindful breathing to enhance self-awareness and reduce stress.

  - Schedule time for activities that nurture your body and mind, like exercise, hobbies, or relaxation techniques.

- **Forgive and Accept Yourself**:

  - Embrace your imperfections and view mistakes as opportunities for growth and learning.

  - Practice self-forgiveness for past errors and choose to learn from them instead of dwelling on regret.

- **Develop Resilience Against Setbacks**:

  - Build resilience by treating failures as lessons and focusing on recovery and progress.

  - Strengthen your support network to provide emotional and practical support during challenging times.

- **Foster Growth Through Self-Compassion**:

  - Use setbacks as stepping stones for personal development.

  - Celebrate small victories and progress towards your larger goals to maintain motivation and a sense of accomplishment.

- **Enhance Mental Health Through Kindness**:

  - Recognize the mental health benefits of self-compassion, including reduced anxiety and depression.

  - Share your experiences and strategies with others to promote a wider culture of self-compassion and mutual support.

CHAPTER NINE

NURTURING MEANINGFUL CONNECTIONS...

AND COMMUNITY

At the core of a truly satisfying life is our ability to create and sustain real, heartfelt connections. These bonds are what keep our communal life vibrant, filling our days with happiness, shared understanding, and a deep sense of belonging. However, as we navigate the swift waters of today's world, with its endless stream of digital interruptions and an all-consuming busyness, holding on to these meaningful relationships proves to be more difficult than ever. It's quite ironic, really; in an age where we're meant to feel connected to everyone at any moment, genuine connections seem to be slipping further away from our grasp.

This situation brings up a troubling problem: loneliness and a constant feeling of being isolated are becoming more common, gradually chipping away at our collective mental health. Even though many of us have hundreds of "friends" online, too often, we find ourselves lacking real-life support when we truly need it. Across neighborhoods and communities worldwide, there's a growing hunger for a true sense of belonging—a desire to be understood, appreciated, and valued not just for what we do but for who we are. This longing highlights how much we miss depth and authenticity in our interactions with one another, as surface-level exchanges just don't satisfy our deeper needs.

In response, the upcoming discussions will focus on the incredible impact that social support has on our lives and how we can better foster genuine connections. We'll look into how adopting empathy, building trust, and showing kindness can lead us back to having meaningful conversations and, ultimately, bring us closer together as a community. By outlining actionable steps towards establishing and keeping authentic relationships—like setting respectful boundaries and choosing in-person meetings over digital ones—this section aims to offer valuable guidance on how to nurture a supportive circle around us. Our goal isn't only to shed light on how to enhance our individual relationships but also to emphasize the significant role each of us plays in creating a warmer, more interconnected society. Through these insights, we hope to embark on a path toward rekindling the essence of true connection and community spirit in our everyday lives.

BUILDING AND MAINTAINING AUTHENTIC RELATIONSHIPS

At the core of a rewarding social life is the art of crafting and sustaining real connections. It's a journey filled with complexities, yet richly rewarding when navigated thoughtfully. To enhance these relationships, certain principles can make all the difference.

Trust is the cornerstone of any strong relationship. It's what allows for open conversations and heartfelt listening, paving the way for deeper bonds. Sharing your thoughts and feelings candidly, along with offering a supportive ear to others, sets the foundation for a lasting connection. As highlighted by relationship expert John Gottman, embracing vulnerability and showing our true selves without fear not only draws people closer but also encourages mutual openness and trust.

Putting time and energy into relationships is vital. Like a garden needing water and sunlight, connections grow with empathy, support during tough times, and celebrating the good ones. Small acts of kindness show how much you value someone, nurturing a shared commitment to the relationship.

Being honest and open with others is a powerful tool for deepening connections. Authenticity leads to emotional closeness, critical for building strong relationships. When we feel safe to be ourselves, it fosters a bond based on truth and understanding. Enhancing authenticity means sharing personal stories, accepting imperfections, communicating needs clearly, and supporting others to be their genuine selves.

Setting clear boundaries is essential for healthy relationships, ensuring mutual respect and preventing misunderstandings. Establishing what's acceptable and respecting each other's limits promotes a balanced dynamic where everyone feels valued. Effective boundary-setting includes clear communication, respecting others' limits, consistency in enforcement, and empathetic negotiation of differences.

The importance of trust in relationships cannot be overstated, as supported by studies like those by Lajunen et al., 2023, especially in romantic contexts. This illustrates the universal need for trust in forming and maintaining close connections.

In an increasingly divided world, fostering authentic connections goes beyond personal benefits, extending to wider societal interactions. The values of trust, empathy, authenticity, and respect offer a framework for addressing larger issues, promoting a more connected and understanding community.

The evidence backing these principles in strengthening relationships reinforces the importance of a thoughtful approach to interpersonal connections. Whether it's deepening bonds with loved ones, building community trust, or navigating political divides, applying these guidelines reflects the power of empathy and resilience in human interactions.

Reflecting on these insights shows that pursuing genuine relationships contributes not just to personal joy but also to the collective well-being of our communities. Interacting with others through authenticity and compassion enriches our experiences and fosters a culture of respect and mutual understanding. As we traverse the complexities of human connections, embracing trust, empathy, authenticity, and respect lights the way to more meaningful engagements.

Do you know why in 2024, Finland was named the happiest country in the world for the seventh consecutive year, according to the World Happiness Report? The sustained happiness among Finns is often attributed to the country's strong social support systems, extensive welfare measures, and the high level of mutual trust amongst citizens. These factors contribute significantly to personal and societal well-being, offering a supportive community that fosters individual happiness. The Finnish model emphasizes not just the well-being of the individual, but the collective health of the entire community, demonstrating how deeply interconnected personal well-being is with the community support one receives.

SUPPORT SYSTEMS FOR EMOTIONAL WELL-BEING

Having folks around you—be it friends, family, or community members—who've got your back does much more than add cheer to the celebrations. It's like laying down a robust foundation that keeps you steady when life's storms hit. It means that when challenges come knocking, you're not out there braving them solo. To weave this safety net, take the first step by reaching out with purpose. Dive into activities where you can cross paths with people who vibe with your interests. Think about signing up for clubs or volunteering. And don't forget to keep the digital bridge strong with those who aren't just around the corner. Remember, the aim is not just to lean on this network but also to be a pillar within it, nurturing a spirit of mutual support and care.

Now, tackling life's bumps sometimes demands more than a heart-to-heart with someone close. When deep-seated issues bubble up, turning to a professional for therapy can be a game-changer in managing mental health and fortifying emotional resilience. Here's a gentle nudge on how to embark on this journey:

- Pay attention to signs that might indicate the need for professional guidance—like being constantly weighed down, battling non-stop gloom, or grappling with anxiety.

- Do some digging to find experts attuned to your specific needs. Don't shy away from seeking recommendations or scrolling through online reviews.

- Be open and true to yourself in these sessions. Therapy is at its best when you're fully engaged.

- Remember, walking through the corridors of self-improvement takes time, patience, and commitment.

Taking steps to pamper and prioritize yourself plays a critical role in safeguarding your emotional well-being. Whether it's carving out moments for hobbies that light you up, embracing mindfulness, or making sure you're well-rested and nourished, such acts of self-love are keystones for harmony. Sprinkling your routine with physical activity can also do wonders for lifting spirits and slashing stress. Set off on a quest to discover what self-care means for you and seamlessly blend these practices into your everyday life.

But don't let the art of giving to others slip through the cracks. Playing a supportive role not only weaves a web of kindness but also cements your place within your circle. Plus, extending a hand or lending an ear has the beautiful side effect of boosting your own mental space and fulfillment. Seize every chance to be there for someone, offering a shoulder to lean on without passing judgment. This give-and-take enriches your life tapestry and bolsters collective strength.

The power of a solid support system in uplifting our emotional resilience and fostering a sense of belonging cannot be overstated. The perks of maintaining meaningful connections ripple far and wide—from better health to increased longevity and enriched quality of life. Evidence piles up in favor of how crucial positive interactions are for both our hearts and bodies. From strengthening ties, reaching out for specialized support, indulging in self-preservation, to aiding peers, each stride forward in knitting this network marks a leap towards a brighter, content life (Kapil, 2020).

Support systems act as both a cushion and a catapult—they soften our falls and launch us into new beginnings. Thus, cultivating these bonds with thoughtfulness, warmth, and a proactive stance is not merely nice to have—it's vital. Yes, it asks for effort, but the paybacks—a steadier emotional ground, enhanced well-being, and richer relationships—are priceless.

CONTRIBUTING TO A POSITIVE COMMUNITY

Lending a hand at local events and volunteering might seem like tiny gestures, but they weave together the fabric of our communities. When we dive into work with others for a common purpose, it's like planting seeds of positivity in our neighborhood gardens. This collaborative spirit nurtures a sense of togetherness and encourages everyone to care deeply about where they live. From volunteering at food drives to sprucing up local parks, every act of kindness not only makes our towns look and feel better but also fills our collective heart with pride.

Here are some steps to start making your mark:

- Look for causes you're passionate about and align with your beliefs.

- Try to carve out some time each month for these activities, even if your schedule is packed.

- Get your loved ones involved. Together, you can make an even bigger splash.

- If you see something that needs doing, why not lead the charge yourself?

When we talk about building a community, words like inclusivity and diversity are at the core of a healthy, vibrant place to live. It's all about creating a welcoming space where everyone, no matter their story, feels like they belong. This means having open conversations about our differences, celebrating various cultures, and making sure everyone has the same chance to lead and participate. These actions enrich our interactions, bringing a kaleidoscope of perspectives that benefit us all.

To foster such an environment, consider:

- Hosting events that showcase different cultures.

- Giving a platform to voices that often go unheard.

- Making sure there's fair representation in community decisions.

Collaboration is the secret sauce to tackling the big stuff affecting our well-being. When we pool our talents, knowledge, and resources, we're capable of amazing things. By working together, we can face any challenge more efficiently than we ever could alone. Whether it's sustainability efforts, educational outreach, or health initiatives, it's our united efforts that bring about meaningful change.

Getting involved in team projects is easier than you think:

- Connect with community leaders and neighbors to identify needs and brainstorm solutions.

- Combine resources to support significant projects that will have a lasting impact.

- Cultivate a culture of teamwork, where every contribution is valued.

At the heart of a peaceful community lies empathy and understanding. When we take the time to listen and appreciate where others are coming from, it leads to kinder interactions and more thoughtful decisions. This approach can smooth over conflicts and pave the way for policies that look out for everybody. Being empathetic means really hearing people out, expanding your worldview, and standing by those who are struggling, showing them they're not alone.

By actively engaging in our communities, we do so much more than beautify parks or organize food drives; we're knitting a tight-knit fabric of purpose and belonging. As we volunteer, champion diversity, collaborate, and practice empathy, we're laying the foundation for a community that stands strong together. This isn't just about solving today's issues; it's about equipping our community with the resilience to tackle whatever tomorrow brings.

The magic of contributing to a thriving community is the chain reaction it starts. Every small gesture of goodwill or initiative taken sends ripples through the community, sparking further acts of generosity. By fostering this cycle of support, we don't only lift others; we uplift ourselves, finding satisfaction in the happiness and prosperity of our fellow residents. This is the essence of community involvement—transforming individual effort into collective triumph, emphasizing "us" over "me."

This commitment to nurturing compassionate and cohesive communities ties in with the necessity for data-driven methods to confront societal challenges. Utilizing solid evidence allows us to pinpoint critical needs accurately and tailor our strategies to be both impactful and fair. It highlights the significance of informed choices that prioritize the well-being of the entire community over merely economic gains.

Imagine a world where every individual's actions are guided by a deep sense of responsibility towards their community. A world where people genuinely care about the well-being of their neighbors, and where the success of the community is measured not just by economic indicators, but by the happiness and fulfillment of its members.

In this world, people greet each other with warm smiles and sincere inquiries about their day. They lend a helping hand without hesitation, knowing that their kindness will be reciprocated when they need it most. Children grow up in an environment where empathy and compassion are not just taught, but lived every day.

This might sound like a utopian dream, but it's a reality we can all contribute to creating. By making conscious choices that prioritize the well-being of our community, we can set in motion a chain reaction of positivity that touches every aspect of our lives.

It starts with small acts of kindness, like checking in on an elderly neighbor or volunteering at a local charity. It grows through open and honest conversations, where we seek to understand and support one another. And it flourishes when we come together to tackle challenges, united by our shared commitment to building a better world for all.

So, as you read on, keep this vision of a compassionate, thriving community in mind. Let it inspire you to make choices that not only benefit you but also uplift those around you. Together, we have the power to create a world where every person feels valued, supported, and connected – a world where happiness is not just an individual pursuit, but a collective journey.

CREATING A SENSE OF BELONGING AND CONNECTION

We all crave a sense of belonging and connection—it's what makes life truly fulfilling. These aren't just nice thoughts; they're necessary for our happiness and mental health. Joining groups or clubs that spark your interest is an amazing way to meet people who share your enthusiasms. It's about discovering your "tribe"—the people who understand you, with whom you can share and grow. Here are some simple steps to start knitting these connections into your everyday life:

- Scout for local groups or clubs that vibe with your interests, be it reading or hiking.

- Take the leap and start conversations or propose gatherings. Everyone's there seeking connection.

- Stay engaged. Real bonds form over time.

- Keep an open mind. You'll find new aspects of your hobbies through others.

Opening up and sharing your stories is another powerful way to build connections and foster a true sense of belonging. When we share our adventures, challenges, and wins, we let others into our lives, creating a space where bonds can strengthen. For building this level of openness:

- Begin with something small. In a supportive setup, share a bit about yourself and encourage others to do likewise.

- Listen with empathy when others speak. Sometimes, being heard is all someone needs.

- Let your guard down. Vulnerability paves the way to closer relationships.

- Celebrate our shared humanity. Focus on what unites us and appreciate the exchange of stories.

Valuing diversity and recognizing everyone's unique qualities within your circle cannot be emphasized enough. It enriches our existence, expands our horizons, and cultivates a welcoming atmosphere where all feel seen and appreciated. To champion inclusivity and understanding:

- Actively seek to understand and appreciate the varied backgrounds and stories of those around you.

- Engage in and promote conversations on diversity and inclusion, seeing them as chances to learn.

- Stand firm against prejudice and bias in all its forms. Be a supporter.

- Work towards creating spaces where everyone feels they can contribute and belong.

Kind gestures, support, and solidarity are what bind communities. Such actions set off a chain reaction, nurturing a spirit of giving and understanding. To nurture this kind of environment:

- Offer assistance spontaneously. Your willingness to listen or lend a hand can make a huge difference.

- Rejoice in the achievements of others heartily. A community flourishes when its members cheer one another on.

- Commit random acts of kindness. Even the smallest act can be incredibly impactful.

- Remember, mutual respect and care are the foundation of any strong community. Always set an example.

Being part of a community, feeling understood, and valuing our contributions significantly boost our happiness and overall quality of life (Bledsoe, 2023). We blossom through connections that resonate with us, and as community members, we hold the power to create spaces where everyone feels welcome and valued.

Recognizing our efforts toward belonging matters immensely. Each step towards inclusivity, every initiative to connect, and each kind gesture adds to the beautiful mosaic of our collective human experience. In moments when the world seems cold and distant, it's these genuine connections and our celebration of diversity that knit us closer, reminding us of our common humanity. Our endeavors not only uplift us personally but also weave stronger, more lively, and inclusive communities.

INTEGRATING PERSONAL INSIGHTS AND COMMUNITY ENGAGEMENT

As we've explored this topic together, we've seen how important it is to build real connections, support each other emotionally, add something good to our communities, and feel like we belong. We started by talking about how crucial true friendships are, not just for us personally but for society as a whole.

Now, as we find ourselves at the end of this journey, we come to a clear realization: being connected to others is at the heart of what it means to be human. Our society is like a beautiful quilt made of kindness, understanding, and help. This quilt offers us a promise – a hope for a caring, welcoming world where everyone feels important and connected.

This idea, although it starts with us as individuals, calls for a wider awakening in our communities. It makes us wonder - how can I contribute to this sense of unity? By putting what you've read into practice, your efforts can start small ripples that grow into big waves, lighting up the darkness and bringing us all closer together.

Personal Example:

Consider the story of Matti, a Helsinki native whose weekly routine includes community sauna sessions with neighbors, family dinners, and volunteer work at a local shelter. These activities aren't just pastimes; they're fundamental components of his social support system, reflecting the Finnish emphasis on community and mutual aid.

Matti's journey to contributing to his community started with small, seemingly insignificant steps. He began by simply greeting his neighbors and engaging in brief conversations. At first, these interactions felt awkward, and Matti doubted whether his efforts would make any difference. However, he persisted, and over time, these small exchanges blossomed into genuine friendships.

Encouraged by the positive relationships he had developed, Matti decided to take his community involvement a step further. He volunteered to help organize a neighborhood cleanup event. To his surprise, the turnout was impressive, and the shared experience of working together towards a common goal strengthened the bonds within the community.

Inspired by the success of the cleanup event, Matti and his neighbors began to organize regular gatherings, such as potluck dinners and book clubs. These activities not only provided opportunities for socializing but also fostered a sense of belonging and support among the participants.

The ripple effect of Matti's small actions became even more apparent when a neighbor faced a personal crisis. The community rallied around the individual, offering emotional support and practical assistance. Matti realized that the strong social connections he had helped cultivate were not only enhancing the daily lives of his neighbors but also providing a vital safety net during difficult times.

SUMMARY

- **Foster Deep Connections**:

  - Prioritize face-to-face interactions to build stronger, more authentic relationships.

  - Engage in active listening and share your own experiences openly to establish trust and deepen bonds.

- **Embrace Empathy and Kindness**:

  - Show genuine interest and empathy in your interactions to strengthen connections.

  - Perform acts of kindness regularly, enhancing both personal relationships and community bonds.

- **Set Healthy Boundaries**:

  - Clearly communicate your needs and limits to ensure mutual respect in relationships.

  - Respect others' boundaries as well, fostering a healthy, balanced interaction.

- **Cultivate a Supportive Network**:

  - Actively build and maintain a support system that includes friends, family, and community members.

  - Offer support to others, and don't hesitate to seek help when needed, strengthening mutual reliance.

- **Engage in Community Activities:**

  - Participate in local events, clubs, or volunteer opportunities to connect with like-minded individuals.

  - Encourage community involvement by organizing or leading activities that promote togetherness.

- **Promote Inclusivity and Diversity:**

  - Foster an inclusive environment by celebrating diversity and advocating for equal participation in community activities.

  - Educate yourself and others about different cultures and perspectives to enrich community interactions.

- **Utilize Digital Tools Effectively:**

  - Use social media and digital communication to stay connected with those far away, but prioritize in-person interactions when possible.

  - Leverage technology to organize and promote community events, enhancing outreach and participation.

- **Enhance Emotional Well-being:**

  - Recognize the importance of emotional support in maintaining mental health.

  - Seek professional help when necessary to navigate life's challenges more effectively.

CHAPTER TEN

THRIVING IN THE PRESENT

CULTIVATING CONTENTMENT AND PURPOSE

Step into the moment, as though you're on the brink of a tranquil lake, where the water's calm surface mirrors the immediate beauty around us. This picture paints the essence of mindfulness and living with authenticity—two incredibly powerful practices that promise to make our lives deeply rewarding. Yet, it's not uncommon for many of us to find these practices just out of reach. We're often caught up in the tangled web of past regrets and worries about the future, missing out on the wonders the present has to offer.

At the core of our struggle is the relentless pursuit of what lies ahead, coupled with the heaviness of our pasts weighing us down. This chase distracts us from appreciating the "now," the sheer beauty of our current existence. Such pursuits create a rift between our real-life situations and where we'd rather be, leaving us feeling unsatisfied and always longing for more. This endless cycle of yearning and looking back or forward steals away the possibility of finding joy in the everyday, making it hard to feel content and at peace with where we are right now.

PRACTICING MINDFULNESS IN ALL ASPECTS OF LIFE

In Chapter 2, we explored the power of mindfulness in daily life, discussing its role in promoting emotional balance, reducing stress, and enhancing our overall well-being. We discovered how integrating mindfulness into our everyday routines and relationships can lead to a more fulfilling existence. In this chapter, we will delve deeper into the practice of mindfulness, exploring how it can be applied to all aspects of our lives, from our personal experiences to our interactions with others.

Mindfulness is like a gentle guide that leads us to fully immerse ourselves in the present moment, helping us to acknowledge our thoughts and feelings without passing judgment. Imagine experiencing life on a deeper level, where you're acutely aware of your surroundings, your emotions, and your inner self. This is about leading a more healthy and fulfilling life by integrating mindfulness into everything we do.

One of the easiest ways to start practicing mindfulness is through meditation. Think of meditation not as a quiet sit-down but as a workout for your focus. It's about honing your ability to keep your attention on your breathing, noticing when your mind starts to wander, and then bringing your focus back without being hard on yourself. As we discussed in Chapter 2, if you find it challenging to maintain focus during breathing meditation, you can try counting your breaths. Start by silently counting each exhalation, beginning with 20 and counting down to 1. If your mind wanders, simply return to 20 and begin again. This technique can help anchor your attention and prevent your mind from drifting too far.

It's this act of returning to your breath that strengthens your mental muscles for both attention and mindfulness. The National Institutes of Health points out that meditation can significantly boost our focus, decrease our stress levels, and increase our overall happiness (NIH, 2021).

But mindfulness doesn't stop at personal meditation. Engaging in everyday activities like eating or walking with full awareness enriches these experiences too. When we eat mindfully, we savor every bite, noticing the flavors, textures, and sensations, turning an ordinary meal into a moment of joy. This not only makes eating more pleasurable but also aids digestion and helps us feel satisfied with less.

By making mindfulness a staple in our lives, we unlock a world of benefits: reduced stress, sharper focus, and deeper satisfaction from our daily interactions. The National Institutes of Health have linked mindfulness to numerous health benefits, including lower blood pressure, better sleep quality, and decreased symptoms of anxiety and depression (NIH, 2021). These advantages highlight mindfulness's role not just in enhancing personal happiness but also as a preventive strategy for various health issues.

Incorporating mindfulness into our social lives can transform our relationships too. By being fully present in conversations, we listen more intently and communicate more thoughtfully. This deepens our connections and fosters stronger, more positive relationships across all areas of our lives.

Practicing mindfulness regularly lays the groundwork for a life filled with awareness and gratitude. It opens our eyes to the beauty in both the ordinary and the extraordinary, enabling us to ride the waves of life with grace and an open heart. This approach enriches our life experience, making every moment worth cherishing.

Embarking on the mindfulness path is a journey unique to each individual, filled with its own set of challenges and triumphs. Some days might be tougher than others, and that's completely okay. What's important is staying committed, treating ourselves with kindness and patience. As we continue down this path, mindfulness evolves from a mere practice to a vibrant way of life, deeply anchored in the now and brimming with possibilities for joy, connection, and exploration in every facet of our existence.

IDENTIFYING PERSONAL VALUES AND LIVING AUTHENTICALLY

Diving into a life that is truly yours, filled with joy and purpose, starts with understanding and living in line with your deepest values. These values are like a guiding star, helping you make choices that reflect what truly matters to you.

Getting to grips with your core values does so much more than just sorting your preferences; it shines a light on the very heart of who you are and the things that drive you forward. Armed with this insight, you can slice through the clutter of what everyone else thinks and make choices that resonate deeply with you. So, how do you start this voyage of discovery and alignment? Here's a roadmap:

- Look back at moments that made your heart sing, those times when you felt completely fulfilled or exceptionally proud. Dive into why these moments felt so profound.

- Think about the times when you were upset or frustrated. Often, these feelings are clues that something important to you was overlooked or pushed aside.

- Reflect on the issues that stir a fire in you. These can highlight your core beliefs.

- Put what you value into your own words. Making it personal makes it real and easier to follow.

When we live in sync with our values, the rewards are immense. Not only do we feel more confident and empowered, but we also build stronger, more meaningful connections with those around us. Choosing to live authentically takes bravery and honesty, yet the payoff is undeniable. It gifts us a unique identity, strength against life's storms, and a clear sense of direction. Authenticity nurtures trust, sparks real conversations, and knits together a community where everyone is appreciated for their true self.

But let's be honest, staying true to yourself isn't always easy. The urge to fit in can lead us away from our authentic selves, causing a rift within us that dims our happiness and mental well-being. However, the treasures of living true—like greater influence, deeper relationships, and a firmer commitment to what we love—make every challenge worth facing (O'Neill, 2022).

In a world that often favors fitting in over standing out, embracing your true self might seem like a tall order. Yet, being authentic doesn't mean you're on your own. Rather, it means bringing your whole self to every part of your life—being genuine in work, in love, and in pursuit of your passions. It's about voicing your thoughts and standing by them, even when they go against the current. And it's about owning your actions and sticking to your promises, ensuring you are the same person in every setting, anchored by your integrity.

So how can you start weaving more authenticity into your life today? First, pinpoint areas where you might not be fully being yourself. Are there any hobbies or interests you've abandoned because of other people's opinions? Or perhaps you've taken on goals that don't quite fit with your true desires? Acknowledging these gaps is your first step toward realignment. Then, think about small tweaks you can make to invite more of your true self into your everyday life. Maybe it's reviving an old hobby or speaking out about something close to your heart.

Embarking on this journey towards a life aligned with your values is challenging but incredibly rewarding. It requires reflection, courage to defy norms that don't match up with your principles, and the resilience to stay true to your path. But the outcome is a life that's not just more satisfying, but one that enables you to make a positive impact on your community. Through leading an authentic life, we inspire others to find and embrace their real selves, nurturing a society that prizes depth, integrity, and diversity.

CELEBRATING ACHIEVEMENTS AND PROGRESS

In today's world, where everything happens so quickly, we often forget to take a step back and celebrate our wins, no matter how small. Skipping these moments of celebration can steal our joy and lessen our drive to achieve more. It's crucial to pause, recognize, and enjoy our triumphs as this has a positive ripple effect on our mental and emotional well-being.

Consider the value in acknowledging even the smallest victories in life. Every time we complete a task or reach a milestone, it confirms our capabilities and hard work. Celebrating these achievements goes beyond a momentary boost of joy; it deeply reinforces our sense of accomplishment and energizes us to move forward with enthusiasm. Here's a straightforward approach to incorporate this into your everyday routine:

- Start by setting clear, achievable goals.

- Reflect on your achievements once you reach a goal.

- Reward yourself in a way that's meaningful to you, like enjoying a favorite activity or sharing the news with loved ones.

- Keep a record of your successes, either in a journal or digitally. This log will inspire you when future challenges arise.

Thinking about what we've achieved also greatly boosts our self-esteem and appreciation for ourselves. In a world obsessed with outcomes, pausing to reflect is a powerful act of self-care. It builds a positive self-view and strengthens our belief in our ability to tackle obstacles.

Furthermore, celebrating our milestones and expressing gratitude for our journey enhances resilience. Life's unpredictable nature can be daunting, yet recognizing our past achievements reminds us that we're capable of navigating whatever lies ahead. It shows us that growth and advancement are attainable, despite challenges.

Sharing our successes with others adds another dimension to this ritual. It fosters a sense of community and connection, providing support and recognition from those around us. This shared joy not only amplifies our happiness but also strengthens our relationships. It's a testament to the fact that we're not alone in our endeavors and that our successes can motivate and encourage others too.

To introduce this philosophy into your life and impact those around you, try incorporating celebrations into regular interactions:

- Motivate friends or coworkers to talk about their recent accomplishments in meetings or informal chats.

- Create a space, whether physical or online, where everyone can post and cheer on each other's achievements.

- Show genuine excitement and support for others' victories, reinforcing that all accomplishments, big or small, are worth celebrating.

Embracing and celebrating both significant and minor achievements plays a vital role in creating a rich, fulfilling life. This practice not only improves our personal motivation, self-esteem, and resilience but also bolsters our connections with others, building a supportive and positive network. By integrating celebration into our daily practices, we set the stage for a more contented and appreciative existence—where every progress step is recognized and valued.

Imagine a world where every individual takes the time to celebrate their own and others' accomplishments, no matter how small. A world where people cheer each other on, sharing in the joy of progress and the triumph of overcoming obstacles. In this world, success is not measured solely by grand achievements, but by the countless small victories that pave the way to personal growth and fulfillment.

This celebration-focused mindset has the power to transform not only our own lives but also the lives of those around us. When we make a habit of acknowledging and appreciating the progress we see in ourselves and others, we foster an environment of positivity and support.

So, as you navigate your own journey of personal growth, remember to pause and celebrate each step forward. Embrace the power of appreciation, not just for the big milestones, but for the everyday victories that shape your path. By doing so, you not only enrich your own life but also contribute to a world where every individual's progress is valued and celebrated.

EMBRACING THE JOURNEY TOWARDS LONG-TERM FULFILLMENT

Seeing life as a journey rather than a fixed destination allows us to embrace the present more profoundly and joyfully. It's similar to enjoying the view during a drive, rather than just counting down the minutes until you arrive. When we shift our thinking to greet life's unfolding events with eagerness and openness, we start to value the beauty in simple moments. This change in perspective deepens our connection with the here and now, motivating us to engage with life more fully each day.

True fulfillment isn't found in a single moment but emerges from a mosaic of personal growth, discoveries, and lessons learned along the way. Realizing this helps us to accept life's uncertainties and challenges not as barriers but as essential elements of our voyage. Imagine every uphill climb and downward slope on our path enhancing the overall beauty and depth of our experience, making our journey even more fascinating and valuable. This realization builds resilience, equipping us to handle difficult times with grace and flexibility, viewing them as chances for further growth and enlightenment.

Additionally, being open to change and ready to adjust is vital for moving toward true satisfaction. Here's how to weave adaptability into the fabric of your life:

- Start with welcoming change instead of resisting it.

- Use mindfulness to remain calm and focused amidst change.

- Reflect on how you've adapted to changes in the past, reinforcing your ability to thrive through transitions.

- Actively seek new challenges to test and grow your adaptability, learning equally from both triumphs and setbacks.

This strategy keeps us agile and receptive to life's inevitable ups and downs, enriching our journey with valuable lessons from every experience. Successes and failures alike teach us, molding our continuous quest for understanding and personal development.

Likewise, nurturing an attitude of continual progress, self-improvement, and moving towards our fullest potential is crucial for lasting happiness and meaning. Setting realistic goals and celebrating small victories can greatly influence our sense of accomplishment and direction.

To cultivate such a mindset, consider these steps:

- Pinpoint areas for improvement and set attainable goals.

- Embrace an ethos of lifelong learning by seeking opportunities that enhance your knowledge and skills.

- Maintain a sense of gratitude and awareness to cherish your advancements and stay mindful of the present.

- Build a network of support that inspires and encourages you toward achieving your aspirations.

By prioritizing growth and actively working to refine our skills, we bring ourselves closer to our dreams, leading to a life filled with richer experiences and greater contentment.

Ultimately, committing to the journey of personal expansion and fulfillment guides us to a life that is not only more gratifying and meaningful but also resonates deeply with our core values and ambitions. It encourages us to discover, learn, and flourish amid life's intricacies, transforming all our experiences into pillars of strength and wisdom. This shift in outlook enables us to move through life with resilience, grace, and a continuously renewed sense of wonder and gratitude for our journey.

As we adopt this mindset, we equip ourselves to navigate the swift currents of change and uncertainty that mark our times. We come to treasure the journey over the final outcome, immersing ourselves in our growth rather than focusing solely on specific endpoints. This approach enriches not just our personal lives but also how we connect with the world, promoting empathy, comprehension, and a collective recognition of each person's unique quest for fulfillment.

THE PATH TO A FULFILLED AND PURPOSEFUL EXISTENCE

Throughout our journey in this chapter, we've explored various avenues towards achieving a life brimming with joy and meaning. We started by unpacking the power of embracing the here and now, reveling in the beauty of everyday moments. This exploration revealed that life's richness stems from a series of interconnected steps - from being mindful and true to ourselves, to celebrating our achievements, and gracefully navigating the ebb and flow of life.

What we've discussed is about cultivating an attitude that welcomes all that life offers. It doesn't matter where you are on your personal journey; what matters is your willingness to immerse yourself fully in the present, to stay true to who you are, and to take pride in your growth, step by step.

This perspective might strike a chord particularly with those yearning for a deeper bond with themselves and the world around them. The ripple effects of such a mindset extend well past mere personal fulfillment; they pave the way for a society that thrives on empathy, understanding, and connection.

SUMMARY

- **Embrace Mindfulness in Daily Activities**:

  - Integrate mindfulness into everyday tasks like eating, walking, or communicating to enhance focus and appreciation for the present.

  - Practice meditation to improve mental clarity, reduce stress, and develop a deeper connection to the moment.

- **Cultivate a Mindful Approach to Social Interactions**:

  - Engage fully in conversations by actively listening and being present, which strengthens relationships and fosters more meaningful interactions.

  - Approach social situations with openness and authenticity to build trust and deeper connections.

- **Identify and Live by Your Core Values**:

  - Reflect on experiences and feelings to understand your true values.

  - Make decisions based on these values to lead a more authentic and satisfying life.

  - Use your values as a guide to navigate challenges and make fulfilling choices.

- **Celebrate Personal Achievements:**

  - Regularly acknowledge and celebrate your successes to boost self-esteem and motivation.

  - Share achievements with others to strengthen communal ties and encourage mutual support.

- **Maintain Flexibility and Openness to Change:**

  - Adapt to new situations with a positive outlook, seeing changes as opportunities for growth.

  - Embrace life's unpredictability as a part of the journey, not a disruption.

- **Foster Long-Term Contentment and Purpose:**

  - Set realistic goals that align with your values and take incremental steps towards achieving them.

  - Continuously seek personal growth and learning to enhance life satisfaction and maintain progress towards your aspirations.

CONCLUSION

EMBRACING OUR JOURNEY TOWARDS FULFILLMENT

As we draw the curtains on our exploration of personal happiness and well-being, we reflect on the essential truths we've uncovered together. Throughout this book, we've navigated the complex landscapes of modern life—from the stormy seas of stress to the tranquil paths of mindfulness, each chapter weaving together strategies and insights to guide us toward a more balanced and fulfilling existence.

Our journey has illuminated the powerful role of mindfulness, the strength found in self-compassion, and the warmth of genuine connections. We've discovered that in the midst of our fast-paced, often overwhelming world, there lies the potential to cultivate peace, happiness, and meaning in our lives. We've learned that well-being isn't a distant goal but a continuous process, enriched by each step we take towards understanding ourselves and nurturing our relationships.

It's essential to recognize that the journey of personal growth and well-being extends far beyond these pages. The tools and techniques we've discussed—from cultivating mindfulness and emotional intelligence to building resilience and nurturing meaningful connections—are not one-time fixes, but rather ongoing practices that require commitment and dedication.

As you embark on this path of self-discovery and transformation, remember that even small, incremental changes can lead to significant improvements in your overall well-being. Start by incorporating one or two of the strategies that resonate with you most, whether it's practicing mindfulness in your daily routines, setting boundaries to achieve better work-life balance, or engaging in self-compassion exercises.

Remain open to the process of growth and be patient with yourself. Celebrate your successes, learn from your setbacks, and embrace the unique path that unfolds before you. Keep in mind that personal development is not a linear journey; there will be ups and downs, but each experience offers valuable lessons and opportunities for self-discovery.

To support your ongoing growth, surround yourself with resources and individuals that inspire and motivate you. Seek out books, podcasts, workshops, and communities that align with your values and goals, and don't hesitate to reach out for support when needed. Remember, you are not alone on this path—many others are navigating similar challenges and striving for personal and collective well-being.

As you continue to cultivate self-awareness, emotional resilience, and meaningful connections, you'll find that the benefits extend far beyond your personal life. By embodying the principles of mindfulness, compassion, and authenticity, you contribute to building a more empathetic and supportive society. Your personal growth journey has the power to create ripples of positive change in your relationships, your community, and the world at large.

Let this book be a living reminder that your pursuit of happiness and well-being is not just a personal quest but a contribution to a greater good. By fostering your own health and happiness, you are better equipped to share that light with others, creating ripples of positivity that can transform our world.

Embrace the journey ahead with curiosity, courage, and an open heart. Trust in your innate wisdom and resilience, and remember that every step you take towards greater self-understanding and well-being is a step towards a more fulfilling and purposeful life. May you find joy in the present, purpose in your endeavors, and peace in the knowledge that you are never alone on this path. Together, let's continue to strive for a life not just lived, but well-lived.

Afterword

Thank you for taking this journey with me through the pages of this book. Your thoughts, insights and experiences mean a great deal to me. If you felt this book made a positive impact, I would be honored if you would consider leaving an honest review on Amazon or Goodreads. Reader reviews, no matter how brief, help this book find its way to others who may benefit from its message. You could be a guiding light for someone else navigating life's challenges. By sharing how the book impacted you, you become an architect of another person's growth and healing.

 While I'm not able to respond to every review, please know that I read each one and deeply appreciate you taking the time to share your perspective. If you'd like to connect further, please feel free to reach out through the website www.dchristiansen.com.

Wishing you all the best on your continued journey of growth and self-discovery.

With gratitude,
David Christiansen

CHAPTER 01

American Psychological Association. (n.d.). *Healthy ways to handle life's stressors*. Retrieved from https://www.apa.org/topics/stress/tips

American Psychological Association. (n.d.). *How stress affects your health*. Retrieved from https://www.apa.org/topics/stress/health

American Psychological Association. (n.d.). *Stress effects on the body*. https://www.apa.org/topics/stress/body

Can, Y. S., Iles-Smith, H., Chalabianloo, N., Ekiz, D., Fernández-Álvarez, J., Repetto, C., Riva, G., & Ersoy, C. (2020). *How to relax in stressful situations: A smart stress reduction system*. Healthcare, 8(2), 100. https://doi.org/10.3390/healthcare8020100

Cash, E. (2023). *Stress Management. StatPearls.* Retrieved from https://www.ncbi.nlm.nih.gov/books/NBK513300/

HelpGuide. (n.d.). *Quick stress relief.* Retrieved from https://www.helpguide.org/articles/stress/quick-stress-relief.htm

HelpGuide.org. (n.d.). *Stress Management: How to Reduce and Relieve Stress.* Retrieved from https://www.helpguide.org/articles/stress/stress-management.htm

Mayo Clinic. (2022). *Exercise and stress: Get moving to manage stress.* Retrieved from https://www.mayoclinic.org/healthy-lifestyle/stress-management/in-depth/exercise-and-stress/art-20044469

Mayo Clinic. (2023). *Chronic stress puts your health at risk. Mayo Clinic.* Retrieved from https://www.mayoclinic.org/healthy-lifestyle/stress-management/in-depth/stress/art-20046037

Mayo Clinic. (2023). *Stress management: Learn why you feel stress and how to fight it.* Retrieved from https://www.mayoclinic.org/healthy-lifestyle/stress-management/basics/stress-relief/hlv-20049495

Mindful Staff. (2021). *How to Manage Stress with Mindfulness and Meditation. Mindful.* Retrieved from https://www.mindful.org/how-to-manage-stress-with-mindfulness-and-meditation/

Sparks, D. (2019). *Mayo Mindfulness: Know your triggers for stress. Mayo Clinic News Network*. Retrieved from https://newsnetwork.mayoclinic.org/discussion/mayo-mindfulness-know-your-triggers-for-stress/

UC University. (n.d.). *Six Strategies for Effective Stress Management*. UC Graduate School News. Retrieved from https://grad.uc.edu/student-life/news/six-strategies-for-effective-stress-management.html

University of Colorado Law School. (2014). *25 Quick Ways to Reduce Stress*. Retrieved from https://www.colorado.edu/law/25-quick-ways-reduce-stress

Wellcare Community Health. (n.d.). *Manage Stress and Prioritize Mental Health: Techniques for Well-being in a Fast-Paced World*. Retrieved from https://www.wellcarecommunityhealth.org/manage-stress-and-prioritize-mental-health-techniques-for-well-being-in-a-fast-paced-world

Yaribeygi, H., Panahi, Y., Sahraei, H., Johnston, T. P., & Sahebkar, A. (2017). *The impact of stress on body function: A review. EXCLI Journal*, 16, 1057. https://doi.org/10.17179/excli2017-480

CHAPTER 02

American Psychological Association. (2012). *What are the benefits of mindfulness? APA Monitor on Psychology*. Retrieved from https://www.apa.org/monitor/2012/07-08/ce-corner

American Psychological Association. (2012). *What are the benefits of mindfulness?. APA Monitor on Psychology.* Retrieved from https://www.apa.org/monitor/2012/07-08/ce-corner

American Psychological Association. (n.d.). *Mindfulness meditation: A research-proven way to reduce stress.* Retrieved from https://www.apa.org/topics/mindfulness/meditation

Antioch University. (2011). *An exploratory survey of population nurses' attitudes toward electronic medical records. Dissertations and Theses Collection.* https://aura.antioch.edu/cgi/viewcontent.cgi?article=1593&context=etds

Carroll, A., Hepburn, S.-J., & Bower, J. (2022). *Mindful practice for teachers: Relieving stress and enhancing positive mindsets. Frontiers in Education*, 7. https://doi.org/10.3389/feduc.2022.954098

Forster, P. M. (2017). *Mindfulness and the Quality of Romantic Relationships: Is It All about Well-Being?. Open Journal of Social Sciences*, 5(5), 59-63. https://doi.org/10.4236/jss.2017.55005

Guendelman, S., Medeiros, S., & Rampes, H. (2017). *Mindfulness and emotion regulation: Insights from neurobiological, psychological, and clinical studies. Frontiers in Psychology*, 8. https://doi.org/10.3389/fpsyg.2017.00220

Guendelman, S., Medeiros, S., & Rampes, H. (2017). *Mindfulness and emotion regulation: Insights from neurobiological, psychological, and clinical studies. Frontiers in Psychology*, 8. https://doi.org/10.3389/fpsyg.2017.00220

Jiménez-Picón, N., Romero-Martín, M., Ponce-Blandón, J. A., Ramirez-Baena, L., Palomo-Lara, J. C., & Gómez-Salgado, J. (2021). *The Relationship between Mindfulness and Emotional Intelligence as a Protective Factor for Healthcare Professionals: Systematic Review. International Journal of Environmental Research and Public Health*, 18(10), 5491. https://doi.org/10.3390/ijerph18105491

Kappen, G., Karremans, J. C., Burk, W. J., & Buyukcan-Tetik, A. (2018). *On the Association Between Mindfulness and Romantic Relationship Satisfaction: the Role of Partner Acceptance. Behavioural Science Institute, Radboud University Nijmegen, Postbus 9104, 6500 HE Nijmegen, Netherlands*, 5(9), 1543. https://doi.org/10.1007/s12671-018-0902-7

Keng, S.-L., Smoski, M. J., & Robins, C. J. (2011). *Effects of mindfulness on psychological health: A review of empirical studies. Clinical Psychology Review*, 31(6), 1041. https://doi.org/10.1016/j.cpr.2011.04.006

Mandal, E., & Lip, M. (2022). *Mindfulness, relationship quality, and conflict resolution strategies used by partners in close relationships. Current Issues in Personality Psychology*, 10(2), 135. https://doi.org/10.5114/cipp.2021.111981

Sanilevici, M., Reuveni, O., Lev-Ari, S., Golland, Y., & Levit-Binnun, N. (2021). *Mindfulness-Based Stress Reduction Increases Mental Wellbeing and Emotion Regulation During the First Wave of the COVID-19 Pandemic: A Synchronous Online Intervention Study. Frontiers in Psychology*, 12, 720965. https://doi.org/10.3389/fpsyg.2021.720965

Schuman-Olivier, Z., Trombka, M., Lovas, D. A., Brewer, J. A., Vago, D. R., Gawande, R., ... Fulwiler, C. (2020). *Mindfulness and behavior change. Harvard Review of Psychiatry*, 28(6), 371. https://doi.org/10.1097/HRP.0000000000000277

Schuman-Olivier, Z., Trombka, M., Lovas, D. A., Brewer, J. A., Vago, D. R., Gawande, R., Dunne, J. P., Lazar, S. W., Loucks, E. B., & Fulwiler, C. (2020). *Mindfulness and Behavior Change. Harvard Review of Psychiatry*, 28(6), 371. https://doi.org/10.1097/HRP.0000000000000277

Schuman-Olivier, Z., Trombka, M., Lovas, D. A., Brewer, J. A., Vago, D. R., Gawande, R., Dunne, J. P., Lazar, S. W., Loucks, E. B., & Fulwiler, C. (2020). *Mindfulness and behavior change. Harvard Review of Psychiatry*, 28(6), 371. https://doi.org/10.1097/HRP.0000000000000277

CHAPTER 03

American Medical Student Association. (2023). *Ways to practice self-care with a busy schedule - by BetterHelp.* AMSA. https://www.amsa.org/ways-to-practice-self-care-with-a-busy-schedule-by-betterhelp/

American Nurses Association. (2024). *7 Ways to Create a Positive Work Environment for Nurses.* ANA. Retrieved from https://www.nursingworld.org/content-hub/resources/workplace/positive-work-environment/

Coursera. (n.d.). *What Is Time Management? 6 Strategies to Better Manage Your Time*. Retrieved from https://www.coursera.org/articles/time-management

Friedman, S. (2024). *Cultivating a Healthy Work-life Integration Culture. Knowledge at Wharton*. https://knowledge.wharton.upenn.edu/article/cultivating-a-healthy-work-life-integration-culture/

Harvard Business Review. (2022). *A Guide to Setting Better Boundaries*. Work-life balance. Retrieved from https://hbr.org/2022/04/a-guide-to-setting-better-boundaries

Livingston, B. (2022). *Exploring work-life boundaries. University Human Resources - The University of Iowa*. Retrieved from https://hr.uiowa.edu/news/2022/01/exploring-work-life-boundaries

Marquette University. (2024). *Effective time management for students and professionals. Marquette*. Retrieved from https://online.marquette.edu/business/blog/effective-time-management-for-students-and-professionals

Mountain, T. P. (n.d.). *Time Management: 10 Strategies for Better Time Management*. https://extension.uga.edu/publications/detail.html?number=C1042&title=time-management-10-strategies-for-better-time-management

Northwestern Medicine. (2022). *Health Benefits of Having a Routine*. Retrieved from https://www.nm.org/healthbeat/healthy-tips/health-benefits-of-having-a-routine

Pluut, H., & Wonders, J. (2020). *Not able to lead a healthy life when you need it the most: Dual role of lifestyle behaviors in the association of blurred work-life boundaries with well-being. Frontiers in Psychology*, 11. https://doi.org/10.3389/fpsyg.2020.607294.

SelectHealth. (2019). *Why you need to make time for self-care.* Retrieved from https://selecthealth.org/blog/2019/05/why-you-need-to-make-time-for-self-care

CHAPTER 04

ATD. (n.d.). *Tap Into Your Emotional Intelligence to Resolve Conflict.* Retrieved from https://www.td.org/insights/tap-into-your-emotional-intelligence-to-resolve-conflict

Beheshti, A., Arashlow, F. T., Fata, L., Barzkar, F., & Baradaran, H. R. (2024). *The relationship between Empathy and listening styles is complex: implications for doctors in training. BMC Medical Education*, 24(10). https://doi.org/10.1186/s12909-024-05258-9

Bisignano, A. (2018). *Making love last: The importance of emotional intelligence. GoodTherapy.org Therapy Blog*. Retrieved from https://www.goodtherapy.org/blog/making-love-last-importance-of-emotional-intelligence-0601184/

Bradberry, T., & Greaves, J. (2009). *How to be an Emotionally Intelligent Partner: Focus on Relationship Management*. Utah State University. Retrieved from https://extension.usu.edu/relation-ships/faq/how-to-be-an-emotionally-intelligent-partner-focus-on-relationship-management

Croft, R. L., Byrd, C. T., & Kelly, E. M. (2022). *The influence of active listening on parents' perceptions of clinical empathy in a stuttering assessment: A preliminary study. Journal of Communication Disorders*, 100, 106274. https://doi.org/10.1016/j.jcomdis.2022.106274

Harvard Business Review. (2014). *Manage a Difficult Conversation with Emotional Intelligence*. Harvard Business Review. Retrieved from https://hbr.org/2014/06/manage-a-difficult-conversation-with-emotional-intelligence

HelpGuide. (n.d.). *How to Be Emotionally Intelligent in Love Relationships*. Retrieved from https://www.helpguide.org/articles/mental-health/emotional-intelligence-love-relationships.htm

HelpGuide. (n.d.). *How to Be Emotionally Intelligent in Love Relationships*. Retrieved from https://www.helpguide.org/articles/mental-health/emotional-intelligence-love-relationships.htm

HelpGuide. (n.d.). *Improving Emotional Intelligence (EQ)*. Retrieved from https://www.helpguide.org/articles/mental-health/emotional-intelligence-eq.htm

HelpGuide. (n.d.). *Improving Emotional Intelligence (EQ)*. Retrieved from https://www.helpguide.org/articles/mental-health/emotional-intelligence-eq.htm

Michigan State University Extension. (n.d.). *Active listening and empathy for human connection.* Healthy Relationships. https://www.canr.msu.edu/news/active-listening-and-empathy-for-human-connection

Michigan State University Extension. (n.d.). *Use your emotional intelligence to deal with others in conflict more effectively. MSU Extension.* Retrieved from https://www.canr.msu.edu/news/use_your_emotional_intelligence_to_deal_with_others_in_conflict_more_effect

CHAPTER 05

American Psychological Association. (n.d.). *Building your resilience*. Retrieved from https://www.apa.org/topics/resilience/building-your-resilience

Brooklane (n.d.). *Resilience: Building a positive mindset*. Retrieved from https://www.brooklane.org/blog/resilience-building-positive-mindset

Forrest, S. (n.d.). *Study shows the power of 'thank you' for couples*. *News Bureau*. Retrieved from https://news.illinois.edu/view/6367/772090023

Greater Good Science Center. (n.d.). *How gratitude helps your friendships grow*. Retrieved from https://greatergood.berkeley.edu/article/item/how_gratitude_helps_your_friendships_grow

Harvard Health. (2021). *The importance of showing gratitude to your partner*. Retrieved from https://extension.usu.edu/relationships/faq/the-importance-of-showing-gratitude-to-your-partner

HelpGuide.org. (n.d.). *Gratitude: The Benefits and How to Practice It*. Retrieved from https://www.helpguide.org/articles/mental-health/gratitude.htm

Mayo Clinic Health System. (n.d.). *Expressing gratitude to improve health*. Retrieved from https://www.mayoclinichealthsystem.org/home-town-health/speaking-of-health/can-expressing-gratitude-improve-health

Mayo Clinic. (2023). *Positive thinking: Stop negative self-talk to reduce stress.* Retrieved from https://www.mayoclinic.org/healthy-lifestyle/stress-management/in-depth/positive-thinking/art-20043950

Miller, M. (2021). *Increase Resilience with Three Key Neuroscience Facts + Strategies from Emotional Intelligence. Six Seconds.* https://www.6seconds.org/2021/07/28/increase-resilience-neuroscience/

Rock Bottom Hope. (2023). *Finding Hope in Challenging Times: Strategies for Resilience.* Rock Bottom Hope. Retrieved from https://www.rockbottomhope.org/inspirational-blog/finding-hope-in-challenging-times-strategies-for-resilience

Turning Point. (n.d.). *How do we use hope and optimism to overcome stress?* Retrieved from https://www.turningpointkc.org/programs/resilience-toolbox/hope-and-optimism/how-do-we-use-hope-and-optimism-to-overcome-stress

UCLA Health. (n.d.). *Health benefits of gratitude.* Retrieved from https://www.uclahealth.org/news/article/health-benefits-gratitude

CHAPTER 06

Bożek, A., Nowak, P. F., & Blukacz, M. (2020). *The Relationship Between Spirituality, Health-Related Behavior, and Psychological Well-Being. Frontiers in Psychology*, 11, Article 1997. https://doi.org/10.3389/fpsyg.2020.01997

Centers for Disease Control and Prevention. (2023). *Benefits of Physical Activity*. Centers for Disease Control and Prevention. Retrieved from https://www.cdc.gov/physicalactivity/basics/pa-health/index.htm

Cleveland Clinic. (n.d.). *Integrative Medicine: What Is It, Types, Risks & Benefits*. https://my.clevelandclinic.org/health/treatments/21683-integrative-medicine

GT Behavioral Health Center. (n.d.). *Coping mechanisms for managing stress and anxiety*. Retrieved from http://www.gtbhc.org/coping-mechanisms-for-managing-stress-and-anxiety.html

Harvard T. H. Chan School of Public Health & Brigham and Women's Hospital. (2024). *Spirituality linked with better health outcomes, patient care. Harvard T.H. Chan School of Public Health News*. Retrieved from https://www.hsph.harvard.edu/news/press-releases/spirituality-better-health-outcomes-patient-care/

Noble, D. (2024). *A holistic approach to integrative medicine. Mayo Clinic Press*. https://mcpress.mayoclinic.org/living-well/a-holistic-approach-to-integrative-medicine/

Ross, C. L. (2009). *Integral Healthcare: The Benefits and Challenges of Integrating Complementary and Alternative Medicine with a Conventional Healthcare Practice. Integrative Medicine Insights*, 4(13). https://doi.org/10.4137/imi.s2239

Ryff, C. D. (2021). *Spirituality and well-being: Theory, science, and the nature connection. Religions*, 11(12), 914. https://doi.org/10.3390/rel12110914

Sleep Foundation. (2020). *The connection between diet, exercise, and sleep. Sleep Foundation*. Retrieved from https://www.sleepfoundation.org/physical-health/diet-exercise-sleep

Well Care Community Health. (n.d.). *Manage Stress and Prioritize Mental Health: Techniques for Well-being in a Fast-Paced World*. https://www.wellcarecommunityhealth.org/manage-stress-and-prioritize-mental-health-techniques-for-well-being-in-a-fast-paced-world

Yadav, M. (2022). *Diet, Sleep and Exercise: The Keystones of Healthy Lifestyle for Medical Students. JNMA: Journal of the Nepal Medical Association*, 60(253), 841. https://doi.org/10.31729/jnma.7355

CHAPTER 07

American Psychological Association. (n.d.). *Building your resilience*. Retrieved from https://www.apa.org/topics/resilience/building-your-resilience

American University. (2020). *How to Foster a Growth Mindset in the Classroom. School of Education Online*. Retrieved from https://soeonline.american.edu/blog/growth-mindset-in-the-classroom/

Bouta, J. (2024). *Cultivating a Growth Mindset in Kids: Strategies for Success and Resilience. Hutchinson Public Schools*. Retrieved from https://www.isd423.org/cultivating-a-growth-mindset-in-kids-strategies-for-success-and-resilience/

Center on the Developing Child at Harvard University. (2020). *Resilience*. Center on the Developing Child at Harvard University. https://developingchild.harvard.edu/science/key-concepts/resilience/

Cleveland Clinic. (n.d.). *Stressors: Coping Skills and Strategies*. Cleveland Clinic. Retrieved from https://my.clevelandclinic.org/health/articles/6392-stress-coping-with-lifes-stressors

Colorado State University. (n.d.). *Bounce Back - Academic Wellbeing Program*. https://academicwellbeing.colostate.edu/bounceback/

HelpGuide. (n.d.). *Surviving Tough Times by Building Resilience*. https://www.helpguide.org/articles/stress/surviving-tough-times.htm

Katella, K. (2022). *How to be more resilient: 8 strategies for difficult times. Yale Medicine*. https://www.yalemedicine.org/news/resilience-strategies-pandemic

Mental Health America. (n.d.). *Deal Better with Hard Times*. Retrieved from https://www.mhanational.org/deal-better-hard-times

Parrish, M. (2022). *How to Help Students Develop a Growth Mindset. Good Grief*. Retrieved from https://good-grief.org/ways-to-develop-a-growth-mindset/

Rio Salado College. (2023). *F Isn't the End: How to Bounce Back from Failure*. Retrieved from https://www.riosalado.edu/news/2023/f-isnt-end-how-bounce-back-from-failure

UKNow. (2023). *4 ways to bounce back stronger after a setback. Student News*. Retrieved from https://uknow.uky.edu/student-news/4-ways-bounce-back-stronger-after-setback

CHAPTER 08

Administration for Children and Families. (n.d.). *Tips to Stop Self-Critical Thinking*. Retrieved from https://www.wethinktwice.acf.hhs.gov/tips-stop-self-critical-thinking

Crego, A., Yela, J. R., Riesco-Matías, P., Gómez-Martínez, M.-Á., Vicente-Arruebarrena, A., et al. (2022). *The benefits of self-compassion in mental health professionals: A systematic review of empirical research. Psychology Research and Behavior Management*, 15, 2599. https://doi.org/10.2147/PRBM.S359382

Crego, A., Yela, J. R., Riesco-Matías, P., Gómez-Martínez, M.-Á., Vicente-Arruebarrena, A., et al. (2022). *The benefits of self-compassion in mental health professionals: A systematic review of empirical research. Psychology Research and Behavior Management*, 15, 2599. https://doi.org/10.2147/PRBM.S359382.

Dutes, K. (2021). *5 tips to squash your inner critical voice. Life Kit*. Retrieved from https://www.npr.org/2021/12/09/1062746913/how-to-stop-being-self-critical-and-silence-negative-self-talk

Harvard Health. (2013). *The power of self-compassion. Harvard Health*. https://www.health.harvard.edu/healthbeat/the-power-of-self-compassion

McLean Hospital. (n.d.). *The benefits of self-compassion*. McLean Hospital. Retrieved from https://www.mcleanhospital.org/essential/self-compassion

Ochester, T. (2023). *Mindfulness practices can shift our perspective from perfectionism to self-acceptance and self-compassion. Midwest Alliance for Mindfulness*. Retrieved from https://mindfulness-alliance.org/2023/05/11/mindfulness-practices-can-shift-our-perspective-from-perfectionism-to-self-acceptance-and-self-compassion/

Palacio, L. (2024). *The Power of Positive Self-Affirmations! YMCA of San Diego County*. Retrieved from https://www.ymcasd.org/about-y/news-center/child-development-family-life-people-social-services/power-positive-self-affirmations

Self-Compassion.org. (2024). *Self-compassion practices*. Retrieved from https://self-compassion.org/self-compassion-practices/

Sparks, D. (2019). *Mayo Mindfulness: Overcoming negative self-talk. Mayo Clinic News Network*. Retrieved from https://newsnetwork.mayoclinic.org/discussion/mayo-mindfulness-overcoming-negative-self-talk/

Trosclair, G. (2023). *Self-Compassion: The Evidenced-Based Antidote to Maladaptive Perfectionism*. The International OCPD Foundation. Retrieved from https://www.ocpd.org/articles/self-compassion-the-evidenced-based-antidote-to-maladaptive-perfectionism

Woodfin, V., Molde, H., Dundas, I., & Binder, P-E. (2021). *A Randomized Control Trial of a Brief Self-Compassion Intervention for Perfectionism, Anxiety, Depression, and Body Image. Frontiers in Psychology*, 12, 10.3389/fpsyg.2021.751294. https://doi.org/10.3389/fpsyg.2021.751294

CHAPTER 09

Bledsoe, K. (2023). *The Power of Shared Experiences. The Hill*. Retrieved from https://blog.trevecca.edu/thehill/the-power-of-shared-experiences

Center for Creative Leadership. (n.d.). *How to Build Belonging at Work. Center for Creative Leadership.* Retrieved from https://www.ccl.org/articles/leading-effectively-articles/create-better-culture-build-belonging-at-work/

Elias, M. J. (2016). *4 Approaches to Building Positive Community in Any Classroom*. Edutopia. https://www.edutopia.org/blog/4-approaches-building-positive-community-any-classroom-maurice-elias

Gartner. (n.d.). *Build a sense of belonging in the workplace*. Retrieved from http://caasm.org/build-a-sense-of-belonging-in-the-workplace.html

Greater Good. (n.d.). *John Gottman on Trust and Betrayal*. Retrieved from https://greatergood.berkeley.edu/article/item/john_gottman_on_trust_and_betrayal

Hancock, P. A., Kessler, T. T., Kaplan, A. D., Stowers, K., Brill, J. C., Billings, D. R., Schaefer, K. E., & Szalma, J. L. (2023). *How and why humans trust: A meta-analysis and elaborated model. Frontiers in Psychology,* 14(10). https://doi.org/10.3389/fpsyg.2023.1081086

Kapil, R. (2020). *The importance of having a support system. Mental Health First Aid.* Retrieved from https://www.mentalhealthfirstaid.org/2020/08/the-importance-of-having-a-support-system/

Nair, M. (2020). *Helping the community- Ways to get involved. University of the People.* Retrieved from https://www.uopeople.edu/blog/helping-the-community/

National Institutes of Health (NIH). (2022). *Emotional Wellness Toolkit.* Retrieved from https://www.nih.gov/health-information/emotional-wellness-toolkit

She Should Run. (2024). *6 Ways You Can Make a Positive Change in Your Community.* She Should Run. https://www.sheshouldrun.org/resources/6-ways-you-can-make-a-positive-change-in-your-community/

University at Buffalo School of Social Work. (n.d.). *Developing Your Support System.* Retrieved from https://socialwork.buffalo.edu/resources/self-care-starter-kit/additional-self-care-resources/developing-your-support-system.html

World Happiness Report. (n.d). https://worldhappiness.report

Yılmaz, C. D., Lajunen, T., & Sullman, M. J. M. (2023). *Trust in relationships: a preliminary investigation of the influence of parental divorce, breakup experiences, adult attachment style, and close relationship beliefs on dyadic trust. Frontiers in Psychology,* 14, 10.3389/fpsyg.2023.1260480. https://doi.org/10.3389/fpsyg.2023.1260480

CHAPTER 10

American Psychological Association. (2012). *What are the benefits of mindfulness?* Retrieved from https://www.apa.org/monitor/2012/07-08/ce-corner

Harvard Business Review. (2022). *Celebrate to Win*. Personal growth and transformation. https://hbr.org/2022/01/celebrate-to-win

HelpGuide.org. (n.d.). *Benefits of Mindfulness.* Retrieved from https://www.helpguide.org/harvard/benefits-of-mindfulness.htm

Innovative Resources. (n.d.). *Why celebrating successes is important to our mental health.* [Blog post]. Retrieved from https://innovativeresources.org/why-celebrating-successes-is-important-to-our-mental-health/

Leschber, C. (2023). *The Art of Self-Reflection: Unlocking Personal Growth and Fulfillment.* Retrieved from https://www.romans-12two.org/the-art-of-self-reflection-unlocking-personal-growth-and-fulfillment

Nartova-Bochaver, S. K., Bayramyan, R. M., Chulyukin, K. S., & Yerofeyeva, V. G. (2021). *What It Means to Be Oneself: The Everyday Ideas of Authenticity among Primary School Children and Adolescents in Russia. Psychology in Russia*, 14(3), 1. https://doi.org/10.11621/pir.2021.0301

National Institutes of Health. (2021). *Mindfulness for Your Health. NIH News in Health*. Retrieved from https://newsin-health.nih.gov/2021/06/mindfulness-your-health

O'Neill, K. (2022). *The Importance of Authenticity. Berkeley Exec Ed*. Retrieved from https://executive.berkeley.edu/thought-leadership/blog/importance-authenticity

Silverstone Living Team. (2023). *Lifelong Learning Contributes to Personal Growth and Fulfillment in Several Ways. Silverstone Living*. https://silverstoneliving.org/lifelong-learning-contributes-to-personal-growth-and-fulfillment-in-several-ways/

Tole, I. (2023). *A Journey of Self-Reflection and Fulfillment: Unleashing Desires to Achieve Extraordinary Goals. UX Planet*. https://uxplanet.org/a-journey-of-self-reflection-and-fulfillment-unleashing-desires-to-achieve-extraordinary-goals-d9b9113edc79

University of Minnesota Extension. (n.d.). *Celebrate the small stuff*. Retrieved from https://extension.umn.edu/two-you-video-series/celebrate-small-stuff

Williams, K., Ryan, M., & Johnson, P. (2019). *Personality dispositions and well-being: The mediating role of trait emotional intelligence. Personality and Individual Differences*, 154, 109645. https://doi.org/10.1016/j.paid.2019.109645

ABOUT THE AUTHOR

 David Christiansen is an acclaimed orchestrator and composer who has contributed to major video game soundtracks for over 16 years. His work on high-profile projects for industry leaders such as SEGA, Pixar, Microsoft Game Studios, Supercell, and ZeniMax Online Studios, including award-winning video games like The Elder Scrolls Online, The Witcher 3: Wild Hunt, and the Harry Potter series, showcases his exceptional talent and dedication.

David's credits also include orchestral recordings for Andrea Bocelli's 20th anniversary album "Romanza," featuring the title track "Time to Say Goodbye," and the Golden Melody Award-winning album "Winter Endless" by Sodagreen. His production music albums are featured internationally on television.

Navigating the intense pressure and demands of the music industry, David has developed a keen understanding of focus, resilience, and peak performance. His ability to maintain calm, presence, and creative flow during high-stakes recording sessions is a hallmark of his work.

David's journey towards inner peace and outer success began at age 12, when a life-threatening cycling accident sparked his exploration of mindfulness, self-hypnosis, and spiritual inquiry. Raised in a devout Christian family, he initially channeled his faith and fascination with the mind through church music, studying Evangelische Kirchenmusik and serving as a professional organist from age 14.

During his long-time traveling around the world, David's exposure to diverse cultures, healing traditions, and philosophies of resilience enriched his perspective. His studies of near-death experiences and experiments with sound healing further expanded his understanding. These experiences have informed his daily practices for emotional well-being, clarity, and fulfillment.

In the wellness space, David has composed music for the LUMEUS app's "Power of Emotions" emotional training program, which is available both as a mobile app and in select Audi vehicles. He also created the "Relaxing Retreat" adult coloring book with original illustrations and calming music.

Now based in Hamburg with his wife and three children, David is passionate about sharing the practical wisdom he has acquired for achieving harmony, happiness, and high performance. He believes that with the right tools, anyone can access their inner power and compose a life of success, purpose, and joy.

Achieve Peak Performance
and Life Balance
MOMENTUM
MASTERY
The Modern Blueprint for
Habits and Productivity
DAVID CHRISTIANSEN